Achievement in America

ACHIEVEMENT IN AMERICA

National Report of the United States for the International Educational Achievement Project

Richard M. Wolf

Teachers College Press
Teachers College, Columbia University
New York and London

0395077

Library of Congress Cataloging in Publication Data:

Wolf, Richard M
  Achievement in America.

  Report of a study conducted by the International
Association for the Evaluation of Educational
Achievement.
  Includes bibliographical references.
  1. Educational research—United States.
I. International Association for the Evaluation
of Educational Achievement. II. Title.
LB1028.W6   370'.78'073   76-27715
ISBN 0-8077-2493-0

Manufactured in the United States of America

Acknowledgments

The research reported in this book was supported by the United States Office of Education under Grant No. 9-420540-4503 to Teachers College, Columbia University. Interpretations of results and opinions do not reflect policy of either the U.S. Office of Education or Teachers College, Columbia University.

Professor Robert L. Thorndike reviewed the entire manuscript in draft form and made a number of suggestions for improvements. Ms. Janet Simons served as editor and made a series of excellent stylistic and organizational suggestions that served to strengthen the book considerably. Whatever errors and flaws remain are the sole responsibility of the author.

R.W.

New York, New York
January 1977

Contents

Achievement in America

Chapter 1

The IEA Study:
Plans, Materials,
and Procedures

In 1958 a group of educational researchers from the United States and various European countries began meeting at international conferences to discuss the prospect of collaborative multi-national research. By training, these researchers were empirically oriented psychometricians, sociologists, or other types of behavioral researchers. It was this orientation, perhaps more than anything, that permitted them to overcome problems of language and national culture. The group held several meetings and soon embarked on a modest pilot study that tested the feasibility of coordinating multi-national educational research studies. The results of that study (Foshay, 1962) revealed some highly interesting national differences in level, variability, and pattern of educational achievement and encouraged the researchers to undertake a rather more ambitious and systematic study of mathematics achievement in twelve countries. This second study was carried out between 1961 and 1966 and was reported in two volumes (Husén, 1967).

The technical successes of that study encouraged the group to take several important steps. First, the group incorporated itself in 1967 in Belgium as a non-profit scientific organization, the International Association for the Evaluation of Educational Achievement (IEA). Second, the number of member countries participating increased substantially. Included on the membership roster for the first time were some less developed countries that nevertheless possessed the technical and financial resources to carry out the field work within their own borders for the various research projects. Third, the Association decided to embark on a new multi-national study of student achievement in six subject matter areas. It is this project that has engaged the efforts of hundreds of researchers over the past eight years.

This volume documents the United States' participation in that study and presents the results of a number of analyses of U.S. data that should be of interest to American educators. Although the present work is intended as a United States supplement to the international volumes (Thorndike, 1973; Comber & Keeves, 1973; Purves, 1973; Torney, Oppenheim, & Farnen, 1975; Carroll, 1975), there has been a deliberate effort to include enough background material to enable the reader to gain a rather complete understanding of the project without having to refer to the international volumes (unless, of course, he is specifically interested in results not directly related to the United States).

Upon completion of the mathematics study (Husén, 1967), the International Educational Achievement Association (IEA) Council, the governing body of the organization, which consists of one representative from each participating country, decided to embark on a multi-national study of achievement in a number of subject matter areas. Reasons for this decision included the desire to develop a fairly comprehensive picture of student performance at the elementary and secondary levels of schooling in a number of countries, and the belief that the knowledge and experience gained in the conduct of the mathematics study could be used to considerable advantage.

The IEA Council was aware of the complexities inherent in planning and conducting a multi-subject study, especially since, for some of the subjects, there was no widely-shared view of what was or was not included in the domain of the subject as it was taught at the elementary and secondary levels. Also, the Council was interested in studying a number of related variables of interest such as social background and personal characteristics of students, teachers, and principals, student attitudes, organizational features of schools, teaching practices, and teacher options about their subject and the teaching of it, as well as national policies and practices in the field of education.

The prospect of planning and carrying out such a massive study was sobering. Accordingly, the Council decided to divide the study into two phases. Stage 1 was to be devoted to the exploration of the feasibility of mounting an investigation in each subject area, to the development and pretesting of achievement tests for each subject, and to the development and testing of related questionnaires and affective scales. Concurrently, planning for data collection and analysis was to begin. The initial estimate was that Stage 1 would take two or three years and would produce a full set of instruments and procedures that would be available for use in Stage 2, which was to be devoted to the actual data collection, analysis, and writing up of results.

Before Stage 1 could begin, however, a number of basic decisions had to be made. First, the subject areas had to be selected. This was done in the very earliest discussions, when it was agreed that exploratory and developmental work should commence in Science, Reading Comprehension, Literature, French as a Foreign Language, English as a Foreign Language, and Civic Education. After the developmental work had been completed, a review would be made of the progress in each subject; approval of the Council was necessary before a subject could move into Stage 2. This decision was intended to protect IEA from embarking on the field-work stage with an inadequately conceptualized investigation or poor instruments.

A second major decision was specification of the target populations to be studied. It was initially decided that the target populations should be the same for all subject areas. For the multi-national testing, there would be three target populations:

Population I—all students age 10.0 to 10.11 enrolled in full-time schooling.

Population II—all students age 14.0 to 14.11 enrolled in full-time schooling.

Population IV—all students in the terminal year of those full-time secondary education programs that are either pre-university programs (i.e., university preparatory programs) or programs of the same length.

It was also decided that countries could, as a national option, test a Population III of their own definition that came somewhere between Populations II and IV, usually just before the end of compulsory schooling or at some other major point of student school leaving. The reasons for the selection of these age and grade levels are set forth in detail in the international volumes.

Once these decisions had been made, Stage 1 could begin. Through nominations from people both within and outside IEA, international committees were set up in each subject area.[1] These committees comprised persons from a number of participating countries who had special interest or competence in the teaching or the testing of performance in the various subject areas. The major responsibilities of

[1]The membership list of each international subject committee, along with the names of other personnel involved in the six-subject study, are given in the appendices of the various international volumes.

these committees were to survey the participating countries' teaching of the subject at each target population level, to develop a rationale and instruments for a survey of student performance in the subject, and to specify the kinds of questions for which answers would be sought. (How these committees operated and their relationship to national subject matter committees are described in the various international reports.) In spite of all the preparations, mistakes were made. Many of these were quickly detected and corrected; others were not detected for some time, when corrections were made, often at great expense. A few problems were never fully solved; fortunately, these were usually small problems that did not jeopardize the basic integrity of the study. In the remainder of this report, appropriate cautions will be given when necessary.

Although it was deemed desirable to pretest every item for every population in every participating country, this was not possible because of the enormous burden it would have created for the National Centers. Accordingly, it was decided to pretest each item in at least four countries that represented different languages and educational systems. In some cases, a single pretesting was sufficient to provide enough information to prepare the final versions of the tests. In other cases, a second or even a third round of pretesting was required.

The major products of the international subject matter committees were the achievement tests for the three major population levels to be studied. In Science, Literature, Reading Comprehension, and Civic Education, these tests were multiple-choice achievement tests with special features that made them particularly useful for a multi-national study. In the Reading Comprehension and Literature tests, the passages were drawn from a number of different nations. In the Science, Reading Comprehension, and Civic Education tests, there were a number of items that were common to the Population I and II tests and another set of items common to the Population II and IV tests. These common items, referred to as "anchor items," were included to permit an estimate of increases in performance from one population level to another. In the Literature tests, the same passages and test items were used at both Populations II and IV (there was no testing in Literature at Population I).

The tests in French as a Foreign Language were particularly ambitious undertakings. The committee decided at the outset to test student proficiency in the four major aspects of French foreign language learning: reading, writing, listening, and speaking. Tests were thus developed for each of these four areas for each population in which testing was planned. The sheer technical obstacles that had to be overcome in attaining this objective were formidable. For the listening tests, for example, stimulus material had to be developed and recorded and the recordings distributed to the National Centers, which then had to record the directions in the national language. The national master tapes then had to be reproduced in sufficient quantity for a national testing.

The international committees also developed special questionnaires or sections of questionnaires for administration to students, teachers, and school principals. These questionnaires contained items to elicit information about policies and practices concerning the teaching and learning of the subject, organization and scheduling of classes and study time, and reactions to various aspects of the subject.

At the same time, the international questionnaire committee was developing more general questionnaires for administration to students, teachers, and school principals. These questionnaires were intended to obtain information about students' social backgrounds and personal characteristics, teachers' training and other personal characteristics, general teaching practices, amount and length of training of the school principal, and organizational features of the school. The procedures followed in developing the questionnaires as well as the various attitude and descriptive scales are described in the technical report of the study (Peaker, 1975).

At an early point in the work, the members of the questionnaire committee began to have some doubts about the kinds of questions that were being developed for Population I students. There was a rather uneasy feeling that the questionnaire items perhaps required these students to furnish information they might not possess. Accordingly, an investigation was undertaken to test the accuracy of ten-year-olds' responses to questionnaire items of the kind envisaged for inclusion in the main study. A number of items were organized into a short questionnaire and were administered to judgment samples of 50 to 100 ten-year-olds in four countries: Australia, Finland, Iran, and Sweden. Investigators from the National Centers then personally interviewed the mothers of these students, asking them the same questions that the students had answered in questionnaire form. When the mother's and child's responses were compared, there was a high level of agreement on items that dealt with the present life of the student and his family, e.g., father's occupation, present age, and place of study in the home. Items that were retrospective or prospective in nature, e.g., amount of additional schooling desired, length of attendance in a preschool program, and amount of father's education, showed a low level of agreement between parent and child. Consequently, considerable care was exercised in developing questionnaire items for Population I students so as to include only those kinds of items that dealth with the present life of the student and his home. Concurrently, three other aspects of developmental work were progressing. A National Case Study Committee was formed to develop an omnibus questionnaire to be completed by each National Center, following a process similar to that of the questionnaire committees.[2] The international sampling referee and statistical consultant, with assistance from various IEA and non-IEA personnel, was formulating plans for the sampling and analysis of data.[3] Finally, an international data processing unit began planning and developing the system for handling the mass of data that would be generated.[4]

As each international subject matter committee concluded its Phase I work, a full-scale presentation was scheduled for a Council meeting. At each presentation, the work of the committee was discussed at length and a decision was made on whether the subject would move into Stage 2, the field of study. Approval was not a *pro forma* matter. In several cases, the work of a committee was considered not to be at an acceptable level of quality, and the committee was requested to undertake further developmental work if it wished Council approval. In all such cases, committees acceded to the request. At the November 1970 meeting of the Council, the last one of the subjects was approved for Stage 2 work.

Before the field study could be undertaken, much preparation was necessary. The experience of the mathematics study indicated that gathering information under standardized conditions on an international level could be a complex and, sometimes, hazardous undertaking. Thus, elaborate plans were developed to try to ensure the integrity of the field study.

One of the first steps taken was the designation of a National Technical Officer in each National Center. The National Technical Office was the day-to-day operating head of the study within the country. It was felt that the designation of such individuals was crucial to the success of the field work for two reasons. First, the Council members already carried heavy responsibilities that did not allow them the requisite amount of time to donate to managing the project. Second, the amount of detailed work that would be involved in the administra-

[2]See Passow, Noah, and Eckstein (1975).
[3]See Peaker (1975).
[4]See Peaker (1975).

tion of the project within each country would be enormous and would require almost constant attention.

A second major step in planning for the field work was the division of the field study into two stages, identified as Stage 2 and Stage 3. This was done for two reasons. First, the large number of subjects in which testing was to occur coupled with the complex procedures for data handling within each country would have created an impossible workload for the National Centers. Second, not all of the international subject matter committees had completed their work at the same time. Delay of the field work until all subjects were ready would have resulted in a considerable waste of time for the IEA Secretariat. Thus, it was decided that testing would proceed in Science, Reading Comprehension, and Literature in Stage 2, and testing in French as a Foreign Language, English as a Foreigh Language, and Civic Education would occur in Stage 3. The targeted testing time for Stage 2 was 1970 and for Stage 3, 1971. In all cases, countries were urged to test as close to the end of the school year as possible. The decision to break Phase II of the study into two stages met with unqualified acceptance by all National Centers, the IEA Secretariat, the international subject matter committees, and the Data Processing Unit.

The third major step in planning for the field work was the development of standard procedures for drawing national samples at each population level in which testing was to occur, developing procedures for organizing the field work, and specifying the order and conditions under which the tests, questionnaires, and affective scales were to be administered. The first task was supervised by the international sampling referee, who not only set forth the general principles of sampling and suggested specific techniques to be employed, but who also carried on an extensive correspondence with each National Center throughout the development and modification of its sampling plans until they were accepted. The second task, the development of all procedures for the conduct of the field work, was undertaken by the IEA Secretariat in conjunction with the Technical Director, the Data Processing Unit, and the International Sampling Referee. The final product of these efforts was a set of manuals that specified in detail the steps to be taken by the National Centers, from the mechanics of drawing the sample to the procedures to be followed in returning the data to the international data processing center.

The National Centers Manual included the procedures to be followed in securing the cooperation of schools, sampling students within schools, ordering response forms, packaging and dispatching materials to schools, and the steps to be taken in the posttest handling of data at the National Center, along with instructions for dispatch to international processing centers. The Local Coordinators Manual contained the procedures required for the coordination of the testing within a community; this included specifications on the receipt and storage of materials from the National Centers, scheduling of testing sessions, various forms to be completed, instructions for briefing test administrators and completing the school questionnaire, and returning materials to the National Center. The Manual for Test Administrators contained the detailed instructions for test administration at the same level of specificity as most administration manuals for standardized achievement tests. When a National Center found it necessary to deviate from any procedures, it was supposed to inform the IEA Secretariat.

The fourth major step in the field work phase of the study was scheduling, preparation, and execution of a "dry run" testing exercise. This was envisaged as a dress rehearsal for the main field testing and was done for three reasons. First, the expansion of the IEA from 12 to 22 countries, including some less developed countries, suggested that a number of participating countries would have had rather limited experience in carrying out large-scale surveys. A dry run testing would amount to a crash course in the mechanics of research for these countries. Second, it was felt that all countries would benefit from the experience of a full-dress rehearsal of the field work procedures. Also, if during the dry run some of the procedures were found to be faulty or ineffective, corrective action could be taken before the main testing. Third, the dry run would furnish the Data Processing Unit with data on which to test out the processing system. Delays in processing data from the main testing could thus be minimized and the project would be better able to meet its deadlines for the publication of results.

To prepare for the dry run exercise, the National Technical Officers from the participating countries were brought together for a one-week briefing meeting in the fall of 1968. At this time, matters of procedure were fully discussed and the National Technical Officers returned to their countries prepared to assume the responsibility for the dry-run testing. Similar meetings for the National Technical Officers were held in 1969 and 1970 to prepare for the main testing for Stages 2 and 3, which took place, in the United States, in 1970 and 1971.

Although there was a continuing stream of correspondence between the IEA Secretariat and the National Centers, the focus of activity in the project now shifted to the National Centers, which carried full responsibility for the field work carried out within their national borders.

UNITED STATES PARTICIPATION IN THE IEA PROJECT

The United States was one of the founding members of the International Education Achievement Association in 1958. It has participated fully in all activities of the project since then. In the current study, the United States carried out testing in five of the six subject areas: Science, Reading Comprehension, Literature, French as a Foreign Language, and Civic Education. It did not participate in the testing of English as a Foreign Language for two reasons: first, the tests were developed primarily for countries in which English was not the national language; second, the particular subgroups in the United States for which tests might be appropriate, Spanish-speaking students, for example, differed in so many respects from other groups of second-language learners that the meaningfulness of the results was questionable.

During Stage 1 of the present study, the United States National Center was located in the Department of Education at the University of Chicago. For Stages 2 and 3, Teachers College, Columbia University, in New York City served as the National Center. This section describes activities in the United States during the latter two stages of the project. Stage 1 activities were generally limited to reviewing drafts of instruments prepared by the international subject matter committees and conducting small-scale administrations of pretest versions of instruments.

Activities in Stage 2 in the United States were scheduled to commence with the dry-run testing. Because of delays in funding United States participation in Stages 2 and 3 and the fact that the United States already had a great deal of experience in survey research, however, the United States did not participate in the dry-run testing.

The initial activity in the United States was development of a set of sampling plans for Stage 2 testing. This involved some major decisions. The design for the international survey called for testing the same group of students in Science, Literature, and Reading Comprehension at Populations II and IV. This was done to permit between-subject comparisons of student performance. The amount of testing time that would have been required if each student were tested in all three subjects would have been between 7 1/2 and 8 hours. This was judged to be excessive for the United States. Schools in the United States have a long history of local control, and the prospect of a non-governmental agency obtaining so much student time for an external testing program was considered to be extremely remote. Accordingly, testing at Stage 2 was divided into two separate but intertwined enterprises at Populations II and IV. (There was no Literature testing at Population I.) One part would consist of the Science tests and related instruments; the other would consist of Reading Comprehension, Literature, and related instruments. This would cut the maximum testing time per student to about 4 1/2 hours. The figure was still considered high but it was hoped that it would be possible to achieve the necessary cooperation from the schools. To preserve as far as possible the original intentions of the international survey design, it was decided to draw two separate samples within each selected school. In this way it would be possible to obtain estimates of student performance in each school for all scholastic subjects for the planned between-school analyses.

The development of a sampling plan for the United States necessitated consideration of a number of factors. First, the United States is a large country. Second, the administration of education is highly decentralized (with the exception of Hawaii) into over 22,000 local units. These units vary greatly in size and type, including large city units like New York City, where the schools serve over a million students, county units that may cover a substantial geographical area, and local school districts that may include only a few hundred pupils. Third, there are private and parochial schools that function alongside the public school system. Fourth, a single list of all schools for each of the three populations did not exist. Thus, it was impossible to use the school as the sampling unit.

These considerations led to the adoption of a complex multi-stage sampling design. The first stage of sampling was the community. A complete listing was prepared for the United States comprising (1) all towns and cities of over 10,000 population, and (2) all non-urban counties, as defined by the U.S. Census Bureau. Two items of information were obtained for each of these sample units: (1) median education of the adult population, and (2) median income per family.[5] A combination of these two provided a simple index of socioeconomic status on which the communities could be stratified.

Communities were grouped into several size categories, e.g., county units; towns of 10,000 to 25,000; cities of 25,000 to 50,000; etc. Within each size category, there were three categories by level of socioeconomic status as defined above. Each socioeconomic level for each size category was divided into two strata in most cases—one for public schools and one for parochial schools. In addition, there were separate strata for public schools in cities over one million, Catholic

[5]Figures used were from the 1960 census and some later special Census Bureau Reports. Recent research by Hogan (1970) gives empirical support for this practice.

schools in cities over one million, and private non-Catholic schools. In all, there were 29 strata, which are listed in Table 1. In selecting communities for each stratum, random sampling procedures were employed. Two alternate communities were chosen in the event of non-cooperation.

The second task was that of sampling within communities. In the smaller communities, it was possible, once cooperation was secured, to go directly to the pupil as the second stage of sampling. The schools provided lists of all pupils eligible for testing according to the international definitions of the target populations; students were centrally chosen according to day of the month of birth, regardless of month. For Populations I and II, a generally successful attempt was made to test all students who met the international definitions regardless of the grade in which they were enrolled.

In larger communities, it was necessary to interpose another stage of sampling between selection of the community and selection of the students. This was the selection of a sample of schools within the community unit. Where this was done, local school authorities were asked to list all the schools in judged order of achievement from highest to lowest. This list was then broken into several strata, the exact number depending on the number of schools to be tested in the community, and a school (with a first and second alternative) was chosen from each stratum. Students within each school were selected in the same manner as described above.

Since it was anticipated that obtaining cooperation from communities for the conduct of testing might prove difficult and since the amount of administrative and teacher time that would be required (in addition to student time) would be substantial because of the complex procedures involved, it was decided to pay each school a small honorarium to partially compensate school personnel for their time and efforts.

For the Stage 2 sampling at Populations II and IV, two groups of students were selected in each school—one for the Science testing and one for the Reading Comprehension/Literature testing.

In sampling for Stage 3—the testing in French as a Foreign Language and Civic Education—somewhat different procedures were employed. For the testing in Civic Education, a sampling plan similar to the one adopted in Stage 2 was used. A sample of communities, then schools, and finally pupils was selected for Populations II and IV. Testing was not carried out at Population I.

In sampling for the testing of French as a Foreign Language, another and different set of communities was initially selected. Twice

Table 1

Strata for First-Stage Sampling in the United States

Stratum Number	Community Size	Socioeconomic Status	Type of School
1	Over 1,000,000	All	Public
2	Over 1,000,000	All	Parochial
3	250,000 to 1,000,000	High	Public
4	250,000 to 1,000,000	Middle	Public
5	250,000 to 1,000,000	Low	Public
6	250,000 to 1,000,000	High	Parochial
7	250,000 to 1,000,000	Middle	Parochial
8	250,000 to 1,000,000	Low	Parochial
9	100,000 to 250,000	High	Public
10	100,000 to 250,000	Middle	Public
11	100,000 to 250,000	Low	Public
12	100,000 to 250,000	All	Parochial
13	50,000 to 100,000	High	Public
14	50,000 to 100,000	Middle	Public
15	50,000 to 100,000	Low	Public
16	50,000 to 100,000	All	Parochial
17	25,000 to 50,000	High	Public
18	25,000 to 50,000	Middle	Public
19	25,000 to 50,000	Low	Public
20	25,000 to 50,000	All	Parochial
21	10,000 to 25,000	High	Public
22	10,000 to 25,000	Middle	Public
23	10,000 to 25,000	Low	Public
24	10,000 to 25,000	All	Parochial
25	County Units	High	Public
26	County Units	Middle	Public
27	County Units	Low	Public
28	County Units	All	Parochial
29	All	All	Private, Non-Parochial

as many communities as needed were chosen in the first stage of sampling. All such communities were contacted and asked to report on the extent of French teaching in their schools and, if French was taught, whether they would be willing to participate in the testing. This was done because French, unlike the other subjects tested in the IEA studies, is an optional subject and, in a number of communities, was not offered.

The information on the extent of French teaching in the initially selected communities was used to gain more up-to-date information on the number of students studying French in each stratum in the sampling design. This information was, in turn, used to guide the second and, when necessary, the third stage of the sampling. In contrast to the other subjects studied, intact classes within the schools were selected at the last stage of sampling. When there was only one class of students at a particular population level studying French, as was often the case at Population IV, the entire class group was tested. If there were two or more class groups studying French, one was selected at random.

Due to the technical complexities in testing French listening, writing, and speaking proficiency, it was decided to randomly split the total sample of schools at Populations II and IV into two independent subsamples, stratum by stratum. One subsample took the French Reading and Writing Tests as well as the associated questionnaires and affective scales. The second subsample took the French Reading, Listening, and Speaking tests along with the questionnaires and affective scales. In the latter group, all students were administered the French Reading and Listening tests, but a subsample of at most five or six students in each school was given the individually administered French Speaking tests. This was done to keep the testing time within manageable limits and also to avoid overburdening the international team that would be scoring the French Speaking tests.

In the sampling for all subjects, the intention was to test 30 to 35 students at a population level within a school. This was done for the purpose of having reasonably manageable groups for testing within each school. This practical consideration, however, had to be balanced against a differential sampling fraction within each stratum so that the student weights that would be produced at the analysis stage would not differ appreciably from 1.0.

In addition to the regular international testing, the United States chose to test an *ad hoc* sample of students studying French at the Population I level. This sample comprised about ten elementary schools in generally well-to-do communities that offered a regular French program at the elementary school level. The results for this sample have relevance only for those schools that participated in this testing in the United States.

The general structure of the sampling plans for the United States is set forth in Chapter 2. In the results section, evidence is presented on the extent of agreement between the achieved sample and the designed sample. External data from U.S. Census Bureau Reports are also furnished to make it possible to judge further the adequacy of the sample.

After each sampling plan was developed for the United States, it was submitted to the international sampling referee for review. A brief correspondence was held on certain minor points in several of the plans. In addition, it was possible to discuss some of the details of the U.S. plans directly with the international sampling referee, who was present at all meetings of the National Technical Officers. All sampling plans were officially approved by the international sampling referee.

Once the sample for testing had been drawn, the data collection phase began. Internationally prescribed procedures were followed in the testing; these are described in detail in the various international reports. Once completed, the various response information was prepared and dispatched for processing. As described in the international reports, the scoring of all achievement and affective measures was done centrally. In the case of instruments for which the student recorded his responses on a card that could be read by an optical scanner, scoring was done by computer. In the case of the French Writing and Speaking tests, all scoring was done by a specially trained team of scorers in Liège, Belgium. Thus, once the raw response data were shipped from the United States National Center, they were subjected to the same scoring procedures used for every country's data.

The initial steps in processing all data were carried out by the International Data Processing Unit, located in New York, on an IBM 360/91 at the Columbia University Computer Center. As soon as the data files were created, it was possible to use the files for special analyses for the United States. A large part of what is reported in the remainder of this book is based on the results of these national analyses.

To enable the reader to obtain an overview of the instruments used in the study, Tables 2 through 4 give the full list of instruments, the testing schedule, and the testing times for Stages 2 and 3. Copies of the Science and Literature tests and associated questionnaires can be found in the appendices of the international reports of these subject areas. Although the full set of instruments used to measure Reading Comprehension and Reading Speed are not included in the international volume on reading comprehension, enough illustrative material is presented so that the reader can easily discern the nature of these tests.

Table 2

Instruments, Testing Schedule, and Testing Times for
Stage 2 Testing in Science, Reading Comprehension,
and Literature

Session No.	Time (in Minutes)	Instrument
Population I--Science and Reading Comprehension		
1	30	Science Test--Section A
	30	Science Test--Section B
	15	Science Opinionnaire
2	10	Word Knowledge Test
	15	Student General Questionnaire
	10	General Opinionnaire
3	25	Reading Comprehension Test--Section C
	25	Reading Comprehension Test--Section D
	4	Reading Speed Practice Test
	4	Reading Speed Test
Populations II and IV--Science		
1	60	Science Test--Section A[a]
2	60	Science Test--Section B[a]
3	15	Science Questionnaire
	20	Tests on Understanding Science
	15	Science Opinionnaire
4	10	Word Knowledge Test[a]
	15	General Questionnaire
	15	General Opinionnaire
Populations II and IV--Reading Comprehension and Literature		
1	50	Reading Comprehension Test--Section C[a]
2	50	Reading Comprehension Test--Section D[a]
3	10	Word Knowledge Test[a]
	15	General Questionnaire
	15	General Opinionnaire
4	15	Reading Questionnaire
	4 (Pop. II)	Reading Speed Practice Test[b]
	4 (Pop. II)	Reading Speed Test[b]
	15	Literature Questionnaire
	15	Literature Opinionnaire
5	50	Literature Test--Section X, Y, or Z[c]
6	50	Literature Test--Section W

[a] Different tests were administered to students at Populations II and IV.

[b] The Reading Speed Tests were not administered to students at Population IV.

[c] Sections X, Y, and Z were parallel forms of the Literature Test and were assigned, at random, to students within each school.

Table 3

Instruments, Testing Schedule, and Testing Times for
Stage 3 Testing in French

Session No.	Time (in Minutes)	Instrument
Population I--French		
1	20	French Reading Comprehension
2	20	French Listening Comprehension
3	10	General Questionnaire
	10	General Opinionnaire
Population II and IV--French Reàding and Listening		
1	25 (30 at Pop. IV)	French Reading Test[a]
	25	French Listening Test[a]
2	10	Word Knowledge Test[a]
	10	General Questionnaire
	10	General Opinionnaire
	10	Questions about Learning French
	10	French Questionnaire
Populations II and IV--French Reading, Writing and Speaking[b]		
1	25 (30 at Pop. IV)	French Reading Test[a]
	15	French Writing Test--Sentence Completion [a]
	10	French Writing Test--Composition[a]
2	10	Word Knowledge Test[a]
	10	General Questionnaire
	10	General Opinionnaire
	10	Questions about Learning French
	10	French Questionnaire

[a] Different tests were administered to students at Populations II and IV.

[b] French Speaking Tests were administered to a subsample (4 to 6 students per school) from the French Reading and Writing sample.

Table 4

Instruments, Testing Schedule, and Testing Times for
Stage 3 Testing in Civic Education,
Populations II and IV

Session No.	Time (in Minutes)	Instrument
1	35	Civic Education Achievement Test[a]
2	35	How Society Works
3	20	Civic Education Opinionnaire
4	20	Civic Education Background Question-naire
5	10 10 10	Word Knowledge Test[a] General Questionnaire General Opinionnaire

[a] Different tests were administered to students at Populations II and IV.

Chapter 2

The Achieved Samples

There are a number of ways to describe a sample. One way is to specify the number of schools and students tested in each stratum at each population level in each school subject. These can then be compared to the figures for the designed samples. A second way is to compare the values of certain characteristics of the sample with population values obtained from other sources. Thus, for example, the distribution of fathers' occupations of students in the sample can be compared with similar figures obtained by the U.S. Census Bureau, although census figures for adults may not represent precisely data for parents of school age children. Characteristics that are used for such checking purposes are called marker variables. A third way of describing a sample is to furnish data on the precision of estimates obtained for sample statistics. The most common measure of precision is the standard error. Standard errors based on complex samples are not readily apparent in presentations of results, however, because of the difficulties involved in calculating them.

Tables 5 through 11 present the number of schools and the number of students for whom usable test data were obtained for each population level for each subject. In the Stage 2 testing for populations II and IV, two independent samples of students were tested in each participating school—one for Science and related instruments and another for Reading Comprehension, Literature, and related instruments. In the Stage 3 testing, different samples were drawn for the French and Civic Education testing.

As one compares the designed sample with the achieved sample, one fact stands out—both the number of schools and the number of students are lower in the achieved sample than in the designed sample. In some cases,[1] no school districts participated in the testing. Thus, the

---

[1] Strata 13 and 24, Population IV, Stage 2; Strata 13, 21, and 24, Population II, Stage 2; Strata 1, 6, and 11, Population II, Civic Education; Strata 1, 5, and 10, Population IV, Civic Education; Strata 5, 7, 24, and 28, Population III, French; and Strata 5, 24, and 28, Population IV, French.

Table 5

Structure of U.S. Sample for Population I—Stage 2

Stratum Number	Population		Designed Sample		Achieved Sample	
	Schools	Students (in thousands)	Schools	Students	Schools	Students
1	2,430	433	40	600	13	578
2	430	77	7	105	4	102
3	1,300	147	13	195	11	209
4	2,020	227	20	300	18	306
5	1,430	160	14	210	12	228
6	260	36	2	30	2	38
7	400	39	5	75	1	20
8	290	32	2	30	2	37
9	600	57	5	75	4	79
10	1,200	114	11	165	6	115
11	1,200	114	11	165	10	170
12	900	47	4	60	3	59
13	1,025	85	8	120	2	38
14	1,845	152	14	210	12	238
15	1,230	101	10	150	5	96
16	700	59	5	75	4	78
17	1,560	110	11	165	8	133
18	2,080	147	13	195	10	192
19	1,560	110	11	165	9	175
20	900	65	5	75	4	78
21	1,500	89	8	120	3	60
22	1,500	89	8	120	4	80
23	2,000	119	11	165	4	79
24	900	55	5	75	2	33
25	11,540	323	29	435	22	366
26	26,000	727	66	990	31	720
27	20,170	566	51	765	55	1,060
28	3,000	84	7	105	9	143
29	600	36	4	60	2	40
Total	90,570	4,400	400	6,000	272	5,550

Table 6

Structure of U.S. Sample Design for Population II--Stage 2

Stratum Number	Population		Designed Sample		Achieved Sample		
	Schools	Students (in thousands)	Schools	Students[a]	Schools	Students-- Science	Students--Reading Comprehension and Literature
1	740	415	30	540	15	414	394
2	90	48	4	72	3	61	61
3	295	134	10	180	8	170	175
4	455	293	15	270	12	262	272
5	320	146	11	198	7	150	145
6	55	23	2	36	2	39	36
7	80	38	3	54	1	24	24
8	60	24	2	36	2	36	37
9	130	52	4	72	3	65	63
10	255	104	8	144	4	89	89
11	255	104	8	144	7	143	152
12	125	48	5	90	3	53	53
13	250	81	6	108	0	0	0
14	450	142	11	198	6	214	211
15	300	97	7	126	4	88	89
16	155	42	4	72	2	39	39
17	435	104	8	144	4	118	120
18	580	135	10	180	6	121	128
19	435	104	8	144	5	116	119
20	200	47	4	72	3	72	70
21	520	89	7	126	0	0	17
22	520	89	7	126	3	67	71
23	690	119	8	144	4	94	93
24	85	18	1	18	0	0	0
25	4,680	304	22	396	11	162	139
26	10,540	684	50	900	20	394	392
27	8,200	532	39	702	19	427	430
28	500	32	3	54	3	54	53
29	700	47	3	54	3	58	63
Total	32,100	4,010	300	5,400	160	3,530	3,535

a This refers to the number of students to be tested in each subject (Science or Reading Comprehension).
  The total number of students to be tested is twice the number indicated in each stratum.

Table 7

Structure of U.S. Sample for Population IV--Stage 2

Stratum Number	Population[a]		Designed Sample		Achieved Sample		
	Schools	Students (in thousands)	Schools	Students[b]	Schools	Students-- Science	Students--Reading Comprehension and Literature
1	740	310	30	540	2	42	46
2	90	35	4	72	3	67	69
3	295	100	10	180	8	105	131
4	455	155	15	270	10	164	170
5	320	110	11	198	9	161	162
6	55	20	2	36	2	43	46
7	80	30	3	54	1	23	23
8	60	20	2	36	2	45	46
9	130	40	4	72	3	48	53
10	255	80	8	144	4	90	86
11	255	80	8	144	6	111	114
12	125	40	5	90	4	79	82
13	250	60	6	108	0		0
14	450	110	11	198	4	156	144
15	300	70	7	126	4	86	83
16	155	35	4	72	2	47	44
17	435	80	8	144	2	86	84
18	580	100	10	180	5	90	90
19	435	80	8	144	3	89	88
20	200	35	4	72	1	66	59
21	520	70	7	126	2	44	18
22	520	70	7	126	3	67	37
23	690	90	8	144	3		64
24	85	14	1	18	0		0
25	4,680	225	22	396	7	100	115
26	10,540	500	50	900	12	287	276
27	8,200	400	39	702	19	440	443
28	500	24	2	54	3	71	70
29	700	47	3	54	3	58	60
Total	32,100	3,030	299	5,400	127	2,665	2,703

a Simon and Grant (1970).

b This refers to the number of students to be tested in each subject (Science or Reading Comprehension and Literature). The total number of students to be tested is twice the number indicated in each stratum.

Table 8

Structure of U.S. Sample for Population II Civic Education--Stage 3

Stratum Number	Population[a]		Designed Sample		Achieved Sample	
	Schools	Students (in thousands)	Schools	Students	Schools	Students
1	740	415	21	620	—	—
2	90	48	2	72	1	25
3	295	134	7	200	7	126
4	455	208	10	312	19	452
5	320	146	7	218	6	178
6	55	23	1	34	—	—
7	80	38	2	57	1	29
8	60	24	1	36	1	15
9	130	52	3	78	4	109
10	255	104	5	156	4	116
11	255	104	5	156	—	—
12	125	48	3	72	1	5
13	250	81	4	121	4	109
14	450	142	7	212	7	170
15	300	97	5	145	5	141
16	155	42	2	63	1	35
17	435	104	5	156	5	125
18	580	135	7	202	7	172
19	434	104	5	156	3	85
20	200	47	2	70	2	51
21	520	89	4	133	3	76
22	520	89	4	133	4	108
23	690	119	6	178	3	59
24	85	18	1	27	1	35
25	4,680	304	15	455	12	299
26	10,540	684	34	1,024	13	291
27	8,200	532	27	796	14	345
28	500	32	2	48	2	44
29	700	47	3	70	2	32
Total	32,100	4,010	200	6,000	132	3,232

a Simon and Grant (1970).

Table 9

Structure of U.S. Sample for Population IV Civic Education—Stage 3

Stratum Number	Population[a]		Designed Sample		Achieved Sample	
	Schools	Students (in thousands)	Schools	Students	Schools	Students
1	740	310	20	605	—	—
2	90	35	2	68	1	25
3	295	100	7	195	7	159
4	455	155	10	302	18	467
5	320	110	7	214	—	—
6	55	20	1	39	1	28
7	80	30	2	58	1	33
8	60	20	1	39	1	20
9	130	40	3	78	5	128
10	255	80	5	156	3	88
11	255	80	5	156	—	—
12	125	40	3	78	1	34
13	250	60	4	117	3	79
14	450	110	7	214	7	182
15	300	70	5	136	5	126
16	155	35	2	68	1	27
17	435	80	5	156	5	94
18	580	100	6	195	6	153
19	435	80	5	156	1	27
20	200	35	2	68	2	53
21	520	70	5	136	5	104
22	520	70	5	136	5	123
23	690	90	6	175	3	80
24	85	14	1	27	1	35
25	4,680	225	15	438	11	295
26	10,540	500	31	944	13	276
27	8,200	450	29	877	14	359
28	500	24	2	47	2	42
29	700	47	3	92	2	33
Total	32,100	3,080	199	5,970	124	3,070

a Simon and Grant (1970).

Table 10

Structure of U.S. Sample for Population II French as a Foreign Language--Stage 3

Stratum Number	Population[a]		Designed Sample		Achieved Sample	
	Schools	Students (in thousands)	Schools	Students	Schools	Students[b]
1	740	415	44	1,354	20	751
2	90	48	5	157	3	90
3	295	134	15	437	13	268
4	455	208	22	679	21	446
5	320	146	16	476	--	--
6	55	23	3	75	3	43
7	80	38	4	124	--	--
8	60	24	3	78	3	64
9	130	52	6	170	5	115
10	255	104	11	340	10	208
11	255	104	11	340	9	245
12	125	48	5	156	2	36
13	250	81	9	264	11	175
14	450	142	16	464	11	219
15	300	97	11	317	8	150
16	155	42	5	137	2	42
17	435	104	11	340	11	216
18	580	135	15	441	13	258
19	434	104	11	340	7	158
20	200	47	5	153	4	96
21	520	89	10	291	6	127
22	520	89	10	291	6	153
23	690	56	6	183	4	103
24	85	18	2	59	--	--
25	4,680	122	13	398	9	173
26	10,540	171	18	558	11	190
27	8,200	53	6	173	1	30
28	500	16	2	52	--	--
29	700	47	5	153	4	64
Total	32,100	2,757	300	9,000	195	4,420

a Simon and Grant (1970).

b This is the total number of students tested. The number of students taking the Listening Comprehension and Writing Tests in French is approximately one-half the total number; the number of students taking the French Speaking Test is approximately one-twelfth the total number.

Structure of U.S. Sample for Population IV French as a Foreign Language--Stage 3

Stratum Number	Population[a] Schools	Population Students (in thousands)	Designed Sample Schools	Designed Sample Students	Achieved Sample Schools	Achieved Sample Students[b]
1	740	310	45	1,374	13	386
2	90	35	5	155	3	56
3	295	100	15	443	11	216
4	455	155	23	687	23	385
5	320	110	16	486	-	-
6	55	20	3	89	3	44
7	80	30	4	133	2	34
8	60	20	3	89	2	16
9	130	40	6	177	5	101
10	255	70	10	310	10	195
11	255	80	12	355	10	202
12	125	40	6	177	2	28
13	250	60	9	265	8	125
14	450	110	16	487	13	248
15	300	44	7	195	5	86
16	155	35	5	155	2	28
17	435	80	12	355	9	174
18	580	79	12	350	12	209
19	435	45	7	200	5	58
20	200	35	5	155	4	60
21	520	70	10	310	7	146
22	520	62	9	275	6	107
23	690	30	5	133	2	46
24	85	14	2	62	-	-
25	4,680	104	15	461	9	98
26	10,540	158	23	700	7	77
27	8,200	24	4	106	1	17
28	500	24	4	106	-	-
29	700	47	7	208	3	42
Total	32,100	2,031	300	9,000	177	3,230

a Simon and Grant (1970).

b This is the total number of students tested. The number of students taking the Listening Comprehension and Writing Tests in French is approximately one-half the total number; the number of students taking the French Speaking Test is approximately one-twelfth the total number.

U.S. samples at these population levels cannot be considered fully representative of the age- or grade-defined populations because of the loss of the several strata.

There are a number of reasons for the discrepancies between the designed and achieved samples. First, the tradition of local control of education in the United States combined with the non-governmental status of Teachers College as the National Center made it difficult to obtain the cooperation of local school districts. This meant that a persuasive rather than a directive approach had to be adopted to obtain a national sample. Although a modest honorarium was offered to each school official (administrator or teacher) who had responsibility for the testing, this was not always sufficient to obtain cooperation.

Second, the IEA Project was but one of a number of research enterprises that were requesting testing time from schools at about the same time. The National Assessment of Educational Progress, for example, annually tests thousands of students throughout the country. In addition, the standardization procedures of test publishers, college and university researchers, U.S. Government supported Research and Development Centers, and Regional Educational Laboratories also ask school districts for testing time. In such a context, it is hardly surprising that the present study met with a number of refusals by local school districts that were trying to hold down the amount of time devoted to testing for external projects. Steps were thus taken to coordinate IEA testing with National Assessment testing so that the two enterprises would not be seeking testing time from the same school districts.

Third, some school administrators hold a less than enthusiastic view of the value of research. Such persons often see no direct and immediate benefits from research for the day-to-day instructional operations of schools.

Fourth, the amount of student testing time requested for the IEA study was often considerable. The Reading Comprehension/Literature testing at Population II required four hours and 53 minutes of student time. Similarly, the Science testing at Populations II and IV required 3 1/2 hours. Additional time was required to bring the selected students to a central testing room and to distribute and collect the testing materials. The twin burdens of testing time and special administrative arrangements required undoubtedly led a number of school districts to decline the invitation to participate in the project.[2]

[2]The acceptance rate of first-choice school districts was substantially higher in French than in any other subject, despite the fact that the tests in this area were the most complex to administer. The French Listening tests required a tape recorder to present the stimulus material, and the French Speaking tests required two tape recorders—one to present the stimulus material, the other to record student responses.

Fifth, even after the sample of schools was constituted, often with second, third, or fourth alternates, a number of unforeseen events prevented the testing from being completed according to plan. Some school districts were under federal court order to carry out desegregation plans; this involved shifting pupils and teachers among schools within a locality. The accompanying disruption made it impossible to conduct the testing. There were also teacher strikes in a few school districts. The closing of schools and lost instructional time resulted in some drop-outs from the testing program. Additionally, student uprisings in Spring 1970 resulted in the loss of several secondary schools from Stage II testing.

From the beginning, it was anticipated that the achieved sample would not be identical to the designed sample in any of the participating countries. It was thus decided at the outset to weight all results in the analysis to best represent the performance of each country.

Weighting was done on the basis of population data for each stratum supplied by each country. The weighting procedure that was followed involved the sampling fraction $f_i = n_i/N_i$, where n_i was the number of students tested in the ith stratum and N_i was the number of students in the population in the ith stratum. The general sampling fraction was $f = n/N$, where n was the total number of students tested and N was the total number of students in the defined population. The weight given to each student in the ith stratum was then f/f_i. The sum of the weights over the whole sample was $Nf = n$, the number of students in the sample. When a stratum was not represented in the sample, it was excluded from the weighting process by reducing the population total by the number of students in that stratum in the population. Thus, the sum of weights was still equal to the number of students in the sample.

In addition to the weighting, external checks were made on the quality of each country's sample at each population level for each subject. Each country was asked to identify particular variables included in the instruments whose results could be checked against available census data. Variables used for such checking purposes are termed marker variables. The marker variables used in the United States were sex of student, father's occupation, father's education, and mother's education. National data for these variables was obtained from various reports of the U.S. Census Bureau.

Table 12 lists the percentages of males in the population samples for populations I, II, and IV for Stages 2 and 3. In Stage 2, the percentage of males in the sample is consistently slightly lower than in the population. The breakdown between males and females is nearly equal, however. In the Stage 3 Civic Education testing, the percentage

Table 12

Percent of Males by Population
and Stage

	Population		
	I	II	IV
Pop. (% Male)	51.0	52.7	51.3
Samples (% Males)			
Stage 2--all subjects	49.1	47.1	49.9
Stage 3--Civic Education	--[a]	52.1	51.5
Stage 3--French	42.6[b]	35.9	25.9

[a] Not tested

[b] Special ad hoc sample

of males in the samples at Populations II and IV is virtually identical to the population figures. The Stage 3 French testing shows a marked discrepancy from population figures. Far fewer males are included in the sample than in the school population. This more likely reflects enrollment patterns in French than overall population figures; French is an optional subject in most schools, and enrollment figures in the subject need not agree with overall population figures.

Coding of the father's occupation variable was done using a slightly modified form of the *Dictionary of Occupational Titles* classification (U.S. Department of Labor, 1965). Data were supplied by students on the general questionnaire and hand coded at the National Center. The item was designed to elicit sufficient detail to permit an unequivocal categorization of the father's occupation. That it did not can be seen in the percentages of unclassifiable occupations (see Table 13). For Stage 2 testing, this percentage is greatest in Population I (13.6%) and lowest in Population IV (6.4%).

Among the students reporting father's occupation, the percentages at the higher occupational levels correspond reasonably well with the population figures. The lower occupational levels, however, are underrepresented in the sample. This is especially noticeable in the category Operatives and kindred workers. As Bowles and Levin (1968)

Table 13

Distribution of Father's Occupations for Stages 2 and 3 and Population Percents
for Adult Males in the Population

Occupational Group	Population % Adult Males	Stage 2			Stage 3			
		All Subjects			Civic Ed.		French	
		I	II	IV	II	IV	II	IV
Professional, technical, and kindred workers	12.4	13.6	13.8	11.3	13.4	14.3	21.2	25.5
Managers, officials, and proprietors, including farm owners	17.5	10.8	17.4	22.8	20.7	25.0	23.9	27.9
Sales, clerical, and kindred workers	12.8	11.5	9.9	9.0	8.9	9.0	11.8	11.0
Craftsmen, foremen, and kindred workers	19.9	23.9	26.9	26.7	23.1	20.1	17.9	14.6
Operatives and kindred workers	20.8	7.6	7.1	5.8	5.9	5.5	4.5	3.7
Farm laborers	2.2	2.5	2.7	2.6	5.1	4.9	0.9	0.2
Domestic and service workers	7.1	5.1	4.4	4.0	5.4	5.2	6.2	4.0
Laborers except farm and mine	7.3	2.3	1.9	1.6	3.6	3.0	2.2	0.8
Unclassifiable		13.6	8.1	6.4	4.1	2.7	2.7	2.1
Unknown		9.0	7.9	9.7	9.8	10.4	8.7	10.2

noted, nonresponses are not randomly distributed among groups. Thus, it is quite likely that many of the students who did not report their father's occupation or who provided insufficient detail came from the lower levels of the occupational distribution.

At Population IV, the percentage of students reporting father's occupation at the higher levels is somewhat higher than for Populations I and II. This is likely due to the fact that schooling at this level is no longer compulsory and, of the 25% of the age group who do not graduate from high school, most come from the lower levels of the occupational distribution. This leads to increased percentages at the higher occupational levels.

Information on the amount of father's and mother's education was obtained only from students at Populations II and IV. Unfortunately, the response categories do not coincide with the usual U.S. schooling patterns.[3] For example, a student whose father left school at the end of the tenth grade would be given the same code as a student whose father had two to three years of college.

Median educational levels were computed for each sample at each population level in Stages 2 and 3 (see Table 14). The medians are somewhat lower than for the population at both levels, except for

Table 14

Median Years Father's and Mother's Education

Sample	Father's Ed.		Mother's Ed.	
	Population		Population	
	II	IV	II	IV
Stage 2--all subjects	10.9	10.9	10.9	10.9
Stage 3--Civic Education	11.0	10.9	10.9	10.9
Stage 3--French	11.2	11.3	11.0	11.1
Median Number of Years of Education in the Population for Males and Females Age 25 and over	11.6		11.1	

[3]The categories were (a) 0 years, (b) less than 5 years, (c) between 5 and 10 years, (d) between 10 and 15 years, and (e) more than 15 years.

French. The discrepancy probably arises from the fact that "Between 10 and 15 years" is too broad a category, and underestimates the amount of parental education.

The third way to describe the achieved sample is to provide information on the precision of sample statistics. Such information is necessary to estimate population values. The sampling design was a complex one involving three-stage stratified sampling; simple random sample estimates of error would underestimate the standard errors for a complex sample because there is a clustering effect of students within schools and of schools within strata. The measure used to assess the magnitude of these effects is the design effect (DEFF) (Kish, 1965). For each national statistic computed, DEFF is the square of the ratio of the assessed standard error of an estimate to the expected standard error for a simple random sample of the same size:

$$
\text{DEFF} = \left[\frac{\text{assessed standard error of an estimate}}{\substack{\text{expected standard error for a simple} \\ \text{random sample of the same size}}} \right]^2
$$

Assessments of standard errors of estimates were made using the jackknifing technique (Mosteller & Tukey, 1968). (Full details on the procedures employed and the values obtained for different computed statistics can be found in Peaker [1975], Chapter 2.) The use of DEFF in the following formula allows one to obtain accurate estimates of statistics resulting from the complex sampling design:

Standard error for sample estimate =
Simple random sample standard error $\times$ $\sqrt{\text{DEFF}}$

Extensive computer runs on the IEA sample data have yielded rather stable estimates of DEFF for various statistics—6.0, 2.5, and 2.0 for total achievement test score means, correlations, and regression coefficients, respectively.

Chapter 3

United States Results
in an International Context

Presenting the results of an international study of educational achievement is a delicate matter. The present study was never regarded as an educational Olympics but rather as a research endeavor designed to elucidate the relationships among variables of interest to educators and to develop new strategies and data for comparative education.

It is becoming increasingly clear that researchers have responsibilities to the lay public and not merely to an audience of trained experts, and that these responsibilities are not discharged until the researchers have made serious and deliberate efforts to present and explain their findings in ways that will provide the non-expert with the clearest possible understanding. This point has been made a number of times over during the past few years because of problems associated with the presentation of the results of the IEA Mathematics Study in the United States (see Fattu, 1967, and Romberg, 1971). It has perhaps been most cogently stated by Findley (1975): "The report is out of perspective for failure of the reporters to assume full responsibility for presenting a professional interpretation of their findings to a non-professional lay audience. For mathematics achievement in particular, and educational policy in general, are concerns of the general public in every free nation."

A presentation of the achievement test results must begin with an account of the procedures used in obtaining scores for individuals and how these were aggregated to obtain national results. The achievement tests for each population level in each subject contained between 25 and 80 questions. All questions, except for those in the writing and speaking sections of the French tests, were presented in a multiple choice format with four or five alternatives for each question. Each question was scored as right or wrong. For each examinee, a count was made of the number of items answered correctly and the number of items answered incorrectly; omitted items were not counted in the scoring.

Previous IEA studies had revealed interesting differences in the amount of guessing among countries. In the mathematics study, for example, students in the United States appeared to engage in a large amount of guessing, i.e., a substantial number of questions were incorrectly answered and relatively few were omitted. In contrast, Belgian students appeared to engage in very little guessing; that is, relatively few items were answered incorrectly but a substantial number of items were omitted. Belgian students, it was learned, are taught from the beginning of their school careers not to attempt to answer a question unless they are almost certain they know the answer. This is not true in the U.S., however, where guessing is often encouraged. Such differences in the propensity to guess can affect test performance substantially. The more items an examinee guesses at in a multiple choice situation, the more items he is likely to get right. For this reason, it was decided to use a correction for guessing in determining individual scores. The formula employed was the conventional one:

$$S = R - \frac{W}{k-1}$$

where S is the individual's corrected score,
   R is the number of questions answered correctly,
   W is the number of questions answered incorrectly (omitted items not counted), and
   k is the number of alternative choices for each question, usually 4 or 5.

This correction for guessing was intended to minimize the effects of guessing.

Once the corrected score for each student was obtained, it was possible to compute each country's weighted mean and standard deviation. These weighted statistics were computed to best represent each country's performance.

The results of each population in each scholastic subject in which the United States tested are presented in Figures 1 through 8. The format for each figure is the same. Each participating country's performance at each population level is expressed in standard deviation units from the United States mean based on the U.S. standard deviation for that group as a unit. That is, the United States mean was subtracted from each other country's mean and the difference divided by the United States standard deviation. Thus, a mark at $+0.5$ denotes that a country's mean was one-half standard deviation *above* the United States mean; similarly, a mark at -0.5 indicates that a country's mean is one-half standard deviation *below* the United States mean at a given population level in a given subject. The number of countries having means above and below the United States mean at a given population level in a subject can be easily obtained by counting the number of marks above and below the zero point, the United States mean.

The results for Populations I and II can be interpreted relatively easily from the figures. Populations I and II represent age levels at which schooling is compulsory in all the participating countries. One must bear in mind, however, that similar age groups do not mean similar amounts of schooling. Specifically, schooling begins at age 5 in Australia, England, New Zealand, and Scotland, whereas it does not begin until age 7 in Chile, Finland, the Netherlands, and Sweden. In the remaining countries, schooling begins at age 6.

The results for Population IV, on the other hand, must be interpreted with extreme caution. These students are from a level at which schooling is not compulsory. Estimates submitted by the participating countries showed that the percent of an age group enrolled in full-time schooling at the Population IV level ranged from 9% in the Federal Republic of Germany and Iran to 75% in the United States (see Table 15).

The United States retains a greater proportion of an age group in full-time schooling than does any other participating country. One consequence of this is to lower the average achievement at the Population IV level because a relatively unselected group of students is being brought to the end of secondary education; in many other countries, however, conscious selection processes operate to retain only the most able students.

The following procedure was employed in estimating the performance of comparable proportions of the age group at Population IV. First, each participating country submitted its national estimate of the percent of an age group completing secondary education. The countries with the *lowest* proportion of students at the Population IV level (the Federal Republic of Germany and Iran) were used to establish the proportion of the age group that would be included in the analysis. That fraction of the upper part of each country's weighted score distribution in each subject that would represent the top 9% of the *age group* was identified and the mean and standard deviation computed for the tail of the original distribution. Thus, if a country had 18% of an

Table 15

Percent of Age Group Enrolled in Full-time
Schooling in the Terminal Year of Secondary School

Country	Percent
Australia	29
Belgium (Flemish)	47
Belgium (French)	47
Chile	16
England	20
Federal Republic of Germany	9
Finland	21
France	29
Hungary	28
India	14
Iran	9
Italy	16
Netherlands	13
New Zealand	13
Scotland	17
Sweden	45
Thailand	10
United States	75

age group completing secondary education, the top half of its sample score distribution would be included in the analysis, whereas a country that reported 36% of an age group completing secondary education would have the top quarter of its score distribution included in the computations. In the case of the United States, the top of the weighted score distribution was used in the computations.

The difference between each country's mean for the estimated 9% of the age group and the United States mean for the estimated top 9% of the age group was obtained and divided by the U.S. Population IV standard deviation. These results, expressed in U.S. standard deviation units, are also presented in Figures 1 through 8.

This procedure can be criticized on the grounds that it gives undue advantage to countries with greater retention. No selection procedure works perfectly and a country with 9% of an age group at the end of secondary school will almost certainly not have the best 9%, although it is likely that most students will be correctly placed in that group. The procedure of waiting until after the test to select the top 9% from countries with greater retentivity will therefore produce a higher scoring group than would otherwise be the case.

The reply to this criticism is that the analysis deals with the *actual* products of each country on the tests. From their actual 9%, countries with lower retention rates produce a certain level of score. From their larger 20%, 40%, or even 75% other countries can extract a best-scoring subgroup of 9% producing various mean scores. Unfortunately, there is no way to estimate the amount of inflation in the scores for the top 9% of the age group in the countries with greater retention. Thus, the true levels of performance at the end of secondary school probably lie somewhere between the actual Population IV results and the results for the estimated 9% of the age group.

With the above qualifications in mind, we can turn to the figures presenting the results. Figure 1 presents the U.S. results in relation to the other countries' performance in science. For Population I, three countries had higher mean scores than did the United States; these were +0.02, +0.06, and +0.43 standard deviation units above the United States mean.

At Population II, seven countries' means exceeded the U.S. mean by from 0.02 to 0.84 U.S. standard deviation units. Ten countries had means that were lower than the U.S. mean. These ranged from −.01 to −1.20 U.S. standard deviation units. These results, however, require some qualification. Population II was defined as students between age 14.0 and 14.11 who were enrolled in full-time schooling. This level was selected for two reasons. First, it is the last age in which schooling

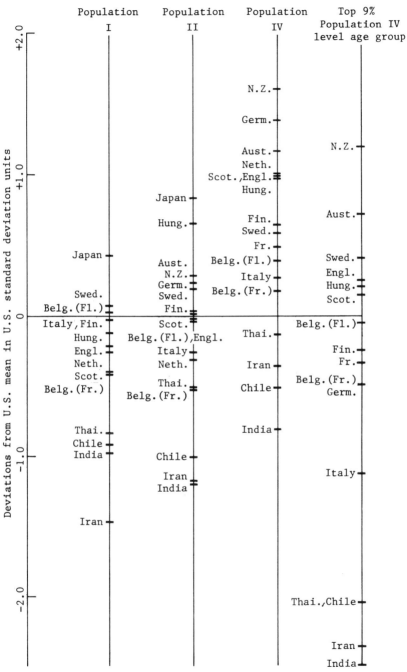

Figure 1   Science

was officially required in all the participating countries and, second, instruction is given by teachers who are specially trained in the teaching of each subject rather than by a general classroom teacher. After the study was underway, however, it was discovered that not all the individuals in the age group were enrolled in full-time schooling. In some of the low income countries, e.g., India and Iran, as few as 25% of the students were actually enrolled in full-time schooling. Thus, it is possible that part of the U.S.'s lower relative standing at Population II might be because of selection factors operating in other countries.

The results for Population IV require special care in interpretation. The first set of results for Population IV presented in Figure 1 shows that thirteen countries had higher means than the United States, ranging from +0.17 to +1.61 U.S. standard deviation units. Four countries had means lower than the U.S. mean, ranging from −0.14 to −0.81 U.S. standard deviation units. These results, however, do not take into account the differential proportions of the age group still in school at the Population IV level. The last column in Figure 1 attempts to do this. Here, estimates of performance of the top 9% of the age group are presented. They are subject to the qualifications presented earlier. The results indicate that six countries had means greater than the United States, and eleven were lower. This is in marked contrast to the full Population IV results. Of the six countries with means higher than the U.S., the range of performance is from 0.20 to 1.19 standard deviation units; for the countries with means below the U.S., the range is from −0.06 to −2.49 standard deviation units. The four countries that are most discrepant from the U.S. (−2.06, −2.06, −2.36, and −2.49) are all low income countries.

It is somewhat difficult to summarize the overall science achievement test results. At Population I, the U.S. mean was among the highest. The results at Population II were somewhat similar, although the relative standing of the U.S. was lower. At Population IV, the U.S. mean, as expected, was among the lowest but the picture changed dramatically when the results for the estimated top 9% of the age group were examined. It is quite clear, however, that even for this last analysis, several countries showed substantially[1] higher average performance than did the U.S., and several were notably lower.

---

[1]Although it is possible to determine the statistical significance of these differences, this is of questionable value in the IEA study. Statistical significance is, to a large extent, a function of sample size. The larger the sample size, the more likely a difference is to be statistically significant. In the present study, given the enormous sample sizes, almost any difference, no matter how small, is likely to be statistically significant. Thus, the usual tests of significance have been dispensed with and attention focused on the meaningfulness of differences.

One more caution must be introduced that is particularly germane to the science achievement testing. Simply stated, it is that there is considerable variation in the amount of opportunity afforded students to learn the material included in the test. The procedure followed was to have a group of teachers in each school meet and rate each item in the test according to the following scale:

1. None of the students in the appropriate age (or grade) group has studied the topic embodied in this item.
2. Fewer than 25% of the students in the appropriate age (or grade) group have studied the topic embodied in this item.
3. Between 25% and 75% of the students in the appropriate age (or grade) group have studied the topic embodied in this item.
4. More than 75% of the students in the appropriate age (or grade) group have studied the topic embodied in this item.
5. All the students in the appropriate age (or grade) group have studied the topic embodied in this item.

This rating was done separately at each population level. The ratings were returned along with the test materials and included in the data processing. From the rating data, a national opportunity-to-learn score was obtained for each school; these were then aggregated to determine an overall rating for each country at each population level. The rank order correlations between opportunity to learn science and achievement, across countries, are $+.51$, $+.75$, and $+.36$ for Populations I, II, and IV, respectively. This indicates that in those countries where students had greater opportunity to learn what was included in the test, performance was higher.

As shown in Table 16, the relative standing of the United States in opportunity to learn and in science achievement is quite close at all levels. Interestingly, as one moves from Population I to Population II, the relative standing of the U.S. decreases for both opportunity and achievement. This indicates an increasing divergence between the material included in the test and what students in the U.S. are learning in science and also the test performance of the U.S. students. At Population IV, the rather low relative standing of the U.S. on both opportunity and achievement is probably a function both of the lack of selection and of the relative lack of specialization in science.

Reading Comprehension results are presented in Figure 2. 14 countries tested in this subject at Population I and 15 countries at Populations II and IV. At Population I, eight countries had means higher than the United States, five lower. For countries having means

Table 16

United States Rank Order in Opportunity to Learn and
Science Achievement at Populations I, II, and IV

Population	Rank order of United States in		No. of Countries Testing and Rating Opportunity to Learn
	Opportunity to Learn	Science Achievement	
I	1	4	14
II	6	7	16
IV	13	14	16

greater than the U.S., the range was from 0.06 to 0.41 standard deviation units; for countries having means lower than the U.S., the range was from -0.23 to -1.13. At Population II, two countries had means higher than the U.S. ($+.06$ and $+.17$ standard deviation units), and twelve had means lower than the U.S. (-0.01 to -1.68 standard deviation units). The notable feature of the results for the two populations is the apparent closeness of the national means. At Population II, eight countries' means lie between 0.30 and -0.30 standard deviation units of the U.S. mean; at Population II, eleven countries' means fall between $+0.17$ and -0.40. The countries that lie outside the ranges are below the U.S. mean, and low income countries. The sole exception on the high side occurs at Population I.

The results at Population IV were generally as expected. Eleven countries had means greater than the U.S. mean and three lower. For countries with means greater than the United States', the range was from 0.17 to 1.13 standard deviation units. The three countries that had means lower than the U.S. ranged from -0.47 to -1.50 standard deviation units. The estimates for the top 9% of the age group at the Population IV level again furnish a markedly contrasting picture. Here, the U.S. mean was higher than that of any other country. The range of performance of the other countries was from -0.02 to -3.07 standard deviation units. As expected, the two countries with the means that were the most different from the U.S. mean (-2.90 and -3.07) are low income countries.

The results of the Literature testing are presented in Figure 3.

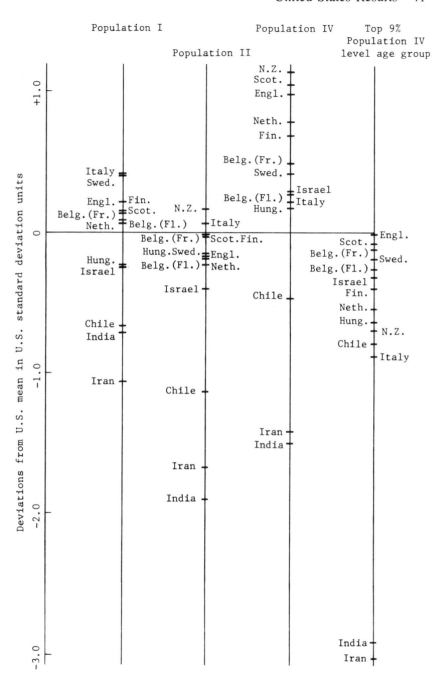

Figure 2   Reading Comprehension

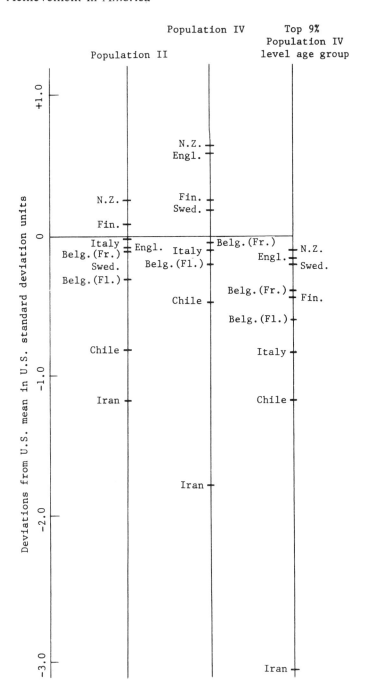

Figure 3   Literature

Testing in this subject was carried out only at Populations II and IV because literature study at Population I is usually limited, somewhat informal, and typically included in the regular program of reading instruction. Testing was carried out in ten countries at both Populations II and IV. At Population II, most countries showed similar results. Seven countries scored within about three-tenths of a standard deviation unit of the U.S. mean: two above and five below. The remaining two countries' means were -0.82 and -1.19 standard deviations below the U.S. mean. Again, these are low income countries. At Population IV, there was a greater spread of national means. Four were greater than the U.S. mean ($+0.18$ to $+0.64$ standard deviation units), and five were lower than the U.S. mean (-0.05 to -1.79 standard deviation units). The analysis of the estimated top 9% of the age group shows a markedly different picture. Here the U.S. mean was estimated to be higher than the mean of any other country. The range of national means was from -0.10 to -3.10 standard deviation units below the U.S. mean. The lowest performing countries were, again, the low income ones.

It is somewhat difficult to explain the results of the Literature testing, although they are not markedly out of line with the results of the Reading Comprehension testing. The actual tests, along with a description of the procedures followed in their development, are presented in the international report of the Literature testing. Of the four passages used in the tests, two are by Americans (William Carlos Williams and Ray Bradbury), one by a Belgian (George Hebblinck), and one by a Spaniard (Ana Marie Matule). It is possible that, since one-half of the passages were by Americans, this may have furnished an advantage to U.S. students because of the possibly greater familiarity with the writing styles of American authors. There is, however, no strong support for this notion. For U.S. students, the item difficulties of questions based on the passages by American writers are generally similar to those of questions based on the passages by non-American authors.

A second possible explanation for the level of U.S. performance might be the form of the items contained in the Literature tests. All items were multiple choice and, although they attempted to test aspects of literary understanding and interpretation, it may be that the item type is quite uncommon in testing literature performance among non-American students.

A third possible explanation, difficult to check, is the quality of the translation of the passages and test items. The international versions of the tests were printed in English and circulated to the participating countries for translation into the national languages. Originally, it was hoped that each country would have one set of individuals translate the tests into the national language and another set of individuals translate the national versions of the tests back into English. The original international version and the back-translated version could then be compared and discrepancies, if any, could be resolved. Shortages of time and manpower prevented this goal from being fully realized; countries generally used all their available resources for the forward translation into the national language. The translations into the national language in a few countries may have been somewhat faulty. This could have serious consequences for the testing because the passages and items contain a number of literary nuances that might be vulnerable to errors in translation. There is some modest support for this possibility. Two other English-speaking countries tested in Literature. At Population II, these countries' means deviated from the U.S. by $+0.25$ and -0.04 U.S. standard deviation units. At Population IV, the two means were $+0.64$ and $+0.58$ standard deviation units above the U.S. mean—the highest scoring countries at that level. In contrast, only one non-English speaking country had a mean greater than that of the U.S. at both population levels. Thus, the possibility of questionable translations must be considered.

Results of the Stage 3 testing in Civic Education are presented in Figure 4. Testing in the United States was confined to Populations II and IV. At Population II, two countries had means greater than the U.S. mean and six countries were lower. The two higher scoring countries were $+.13$ and $+.26$ standard deviation units above the U.S. mean; those below the U.S. mean ranged from $-.02$ to -1.5 standard deviation units. At Population IV, five countries scored above the U.S. mean ($+.42$ to $+.72$), and two countries were below the U.S. mean ($-.46$ and -1.5). When the estimated top 9% of the age group at the Population IV level are compared across countries, one country showed a higher level of achievement than the U.S. ($+0.05$) and six were lower (-0.49 to -3.12).

It is rather difficult to interpret these results. There is considerable diversity in what is taught under the label of "civic education" in the United States. Some curriculum projects have attempted to systematize material in this area but there is no evidence of widespread adoption of such projects. The scope and content of civic education is often locally determined, and there is even a fair degree of autonomy for the individual teacher. Also, students probably acquire a fair degree of information in this area from non-school sources, e.g., TV, newspapers, magazines, etc. For these reasons, it is difficult to draw any implications for the educational system from the test results.

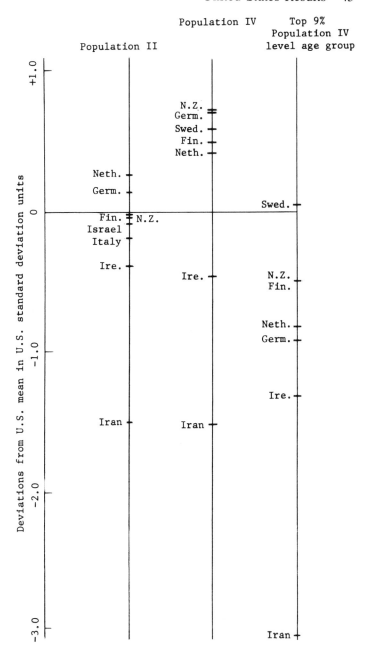

Figure 4   Civic Education

To assist the reader in understanding the results of the Civic Education tests, the major area covered by the test are shown below, including the percent of the total test devoted to each area for Populations II and IV, respectively (Torncy *et al.*, 1975):

1. Fundamental Concepts and Nature of Citizenship—citizenship concepts and definitions of such terms as state, government, patriotism, freedom and responsibility, the rule of law, and democracy (17% and 21%).
2. Political Processes and Institutions—such national topics as constitutions, political history, local government, law making, judicial decision making, executive policy making, and the civil service (17% and 10%).
3. Political Processes and Institutions—such national topics as political leadership, public opinion, elections, and political parties (15% and 12.5%).
4. Political Processes and Institutions—such international topics as foreign policy, national defense, comparative politics, the international political system, and international organizations (21% and 21%).
5. Economic Processes and Institutions—such topics as social services, welfare, taxation, labor organizations, and occupations (19% and 23%).
6. Social Processes and Institutions—such topics as the family, the school, the mass media, traffic, and crime (11% and 12.5%).

Results for the testing in French as a foreign language are presented in Figures 5 through 8. These cover test performance in reading, writing, listening comprehension, and speaking. Although a Population I group was tested in the United States, no results are reported here. There are two reasons for this. First, no other country tested at the Population I level; hence there is no basis for comparison. Second, the U.S. sample at this level was extremely limited and cannot be considered as representative of any larger meaningful population.

There also has been no attempt to estimate the performance of a select top group of Population IV students in the United States in relation to equally select groups in other countries. French is a subject that is taken voluntarily in the United States as well as in a number of other countries. No basis exists for estimating equivalent top proportions of an age group in the United States and the other countries participating in the testing of this subject. One can presume that those students who are enrolled in French at the Population IV level are above average in ability (students at this level have studied French for at least three years) compared to Population IV students in general. One cannot presume, however, that they are the most able students at that level in the United States. The same situation holds true for most other countries.

One point that must be kept in mind when examining the results of the French testing is the years of study of the language (see Table 17). The average number of years of study of French at the Population II level in the United States is 1.8 years. This contrasts with an average of 2.8 years in the other countries testing at this level. The actual range of average years of study is from 2.3 in Rumania to 3.5 in England. At the Population IV level, the average years of study of French in the United States is 4.4 years, contrasted with an average of 5.5 in the other countries testing at this level. The range in these other countries is from 4.3 in Sweden to 7.3 in England. Thus, students in the United States at both population levels have, on average, one less year of French study than do students in the other countries testing in this subject.

Figure 5 presents the results of the French Reading Comprehension test. At Population II, the U.S. students have the lowest mean score of all the participating countries; the other countries range from

Table 17

Average Number of Years of French Study
at Populations II and IV

Country	Population II	Population IV
Chile	--[a]	5.4
England	3.5	7.3
Netherlands	2.5	5.7
New Zealand	2.5	6.5
Rumania	2.3	3.7
Scotland	3.0	5.4
Sweden	--[a]	4.3
United States	1.8	4.4

[a] Did not test at this level.

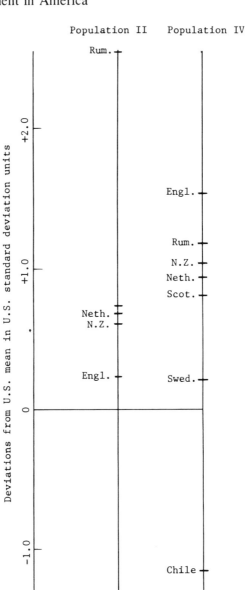

Figure 5 French Reading Comprehension

+.23 to +2.56 standard deviation units above the U.S. mean. Since 52% of the U.S. students in the sample have studied French for less than one year at the time of testing and since initial French teaching tends to emphasize an audio-lingual approach, the low performance of U.S. students at this level is not unexpected. At the Population IV level, the average score of the United States students exceeds only one other country (−1.15 standard deviation units) and is lower than six other countries (+.22 to +1.54 standard deviation units). Since virtually all students in the U.S. sample at this level have studied French for at least three years, one cannot attribute low performance to mere lack of exposure. The greater retention in the United States along with at least an early emphasis on an audio-lingual approach may explain in part the low performance of U.S. students in French reading comprehension. Unfortunately, it is not possible to judge the adequacy of these explanations.

The results for French Writing are presented in Figure 6. At the Population II level, two countries are above the U.S. mean (+.09 and +.49 standard deviation units) and two countries are below (−.04 and −.30). The U.S. performance at this level is somewhat higher than might be expected given the generally low emphasis accorded writing in French at this level. At Population IV, only one country's mean is below the United States (−1.08 U.S. standard deviation units), and six countries' are above (+.18 to +1.05 standard deviation units). The relatively low performance of U.S. students at this level is definite if not readily explainable. Again, one cannot be sure how much of the low performance of U.S. students can be attributed to a lack of emphasis on the acquisition of writing proficiency in French, the greater retention of U.S. schools, or other sociocultural, linguistic, or educational factors.

French Listening Comprehension test results are presented in Figure 7. At the Population II level, U.S. students performed, on average, better than students in two countries and worse than students in three countries. Countries with means below the United States' ranged from −.22 to −1.28 standard deviation units; countries with means above that of the U.S. ranged from +.38 to +2.50 standard deviation units. Except for the country that scored +2.50 standard deviation units above the U.S. mean, for which there is no readily available explanation, the performance of the U.S. students is fairly close to that of three of the four remaining countries.

At the Population IV level, the picture changes somewhat. Two countries have means lower than that of the United States (−.09 and −.92 standard deviation units), and five countries outperform the

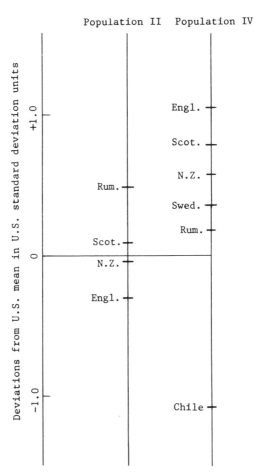

Figure 6   French Writing

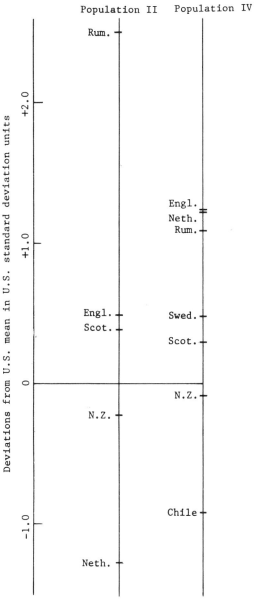

Figure 7   French Listening Comprehension

United States (+.30 to +1.23 standard deviation units). Again, there is no easy explanation for these results. One can only speculate as to whether there is decreased emphasis on audio-lingual methods at the higher levels or whether other factors are operating to impede growth from the Population II to Population IV level.

Results for French Speaking Proficiency are presented in Figure 8. These must be interpreted with extreme caution because they are based on extremely small randomly selected subsamples of students at each population level. By necessity, these tests had to be administered individually and recordings made of speech samples. These were then shipped to Liège, Belgium, and scored by native speakers of French employing a uniform set of international standards. 4% and 5% of the samples of students at Populations II and IV, respectively, were administered the speaking tests in French.

At Population II, two countries had higher means than the U.S. (+.22 and +1.76 standard deviation units) and two were lower (−.10 and −.22 standard deviation units). At Population IV, two countries had lower means than the United States (−.23 and −1.97 standard deviation units), and four were higher (+.17 and +1.19). These results can only be considered as being suggestive and no conclusion should be drawn because of the small sample size in the United States as well as in the other countries participating in this testing.

SUMMARY

It is not easy to summarize the results of testing thousands of students in six scholastic subjects across three population levels. Educators will no doubt be studying the data for some time to come. A modest attempt to summarize is presented in Table 18, which lists, for each subject at each population level, the number of countries whose means were above the United States mean and the number of countries whose means were below. Thus, for example, at Population I in Science four countries had means that were above the United States mean, and eleven were below. Totals above and below the United States mean, across subjects, are given for each population. At Populations I and II, more countries are below the United States mean than above. This is especially true at Population II, where 25 means are above and 41 are below. Since education is compulsory at both of these population levels, the interpretation of results is somewhat straightforward. At Population IV, the situation is of course different. Since the United States retains 75% of an age group in full-time schooling, compared to between 9% and 47% in the other countries (the median for the other countries is 17%), comparisons at this level underestimate U.S.

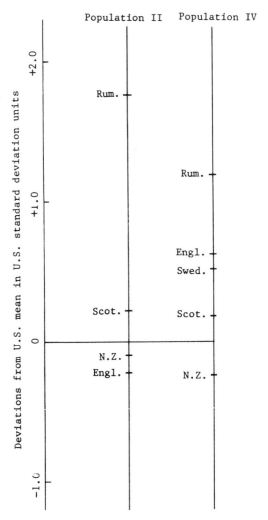

Figure 8 French Speaking

Table 18

Number of Countries Above and Below the United States
Mean in Each Subject at Each Population Level

	Population I[a]		Population II		Population IV		Estimated top 9% of Age Group at Pop. IV	
	Above	Below	Above	Below	Above	Below	Above	Below
Science	4	11	7	10	13	4	6	11
Reading Comprehension	8	5	2	12	11	3	0	14
Literature			2	7	4	5	0	9
Civic Education			2	6	5	2	1	6
French Reading Comprehension			5	0	6	1	--[b]	--[b]
French Writing			2	2	5	1	--[b]	--[b]
French Listening Comprehension			3	2	5	2	--[b]	--[b]
French Speaking			2	2	4	1	--[b]	--[b]
Total	12	16	25	41	53	19	7	40

a Testing at Population I was limited to Science and Reading Comprehension.

b Information necessary to make these estimates does not exist.

achievement. To counter this, estimates of the performance of the top 9% of the age group (as contrasted to the in-school population) have been made. This undoubtedly results in an overestimation of the United States performance, however, because of the high retention rate. The actual performance levels for the United States probably lie somewhere between the two sets of figures. Unfortunately, it is not possible to pinpoint their location with any great confidence. It is likely that the U.S. performance at the end of secondary school is about at the middle of the participating countries.

Chapter 4

Selected Results By Region

In this chapter a considerable body of data are presented for schools, teachers, and students in the United States. In addition, results are presented for the four major regions of the United States—Northeast, North Central, South, and West. This is intended to complement the work of the National Assessment Program, which has reported results by regions for individual test items or assessment exercises, rather than for total test performance. Data on a number of variables about the schools, teachers, and students are also presented to furnish a framework against which test results can be interpreted.

Two cautions must be kept in mind thoughout this chapter. First, region of the United States was not a stratifying variable in the original sampling design. These analyses were done on a *post hoc* basis. This means that the results should not be regarded as precise values, but rather as estimates. Second, all data, other than achievement test information, were obtained from questionnaires completed by school principals, teachers, and students. Such instruments are based on the assumptions that the respondent can answer the questions posed and is willing to do so. Generally, these assumptions are tenable if the questions are not viewed by the respondent as too personal or threatening and if they deal with matters that are familiar. In the present study, this was not always the case. For example, the questionnaire for school principals contained a number of items dealing with educational costs. These yielded a great deal of useless data because a school principal is often not in a position to determine accurately educational costs for his school. In those cases where inappropriate questions were asked, no effort has been made to report results.

Data on the general composition of the sample of schools, teachers, and students for each subject at each population in each region of the United States are presented in Table 19. The composition of each region is as follows:

Table 19

Numbers of Schools, Teachers, and Students by
Region for Populations I, II, and IV

| Group | Region | | | | Total U.S. |
	Northeast	North Central	South	West	
Stage 2					
Population I--Science and Reading Comprehension					
Schools	67	100	44	51	262
Teachers	314	651	289	378	1,632
Students	1,758	1,920	893	877	5,448
Population II					
Schools	34	53	25	33	145
Teachers--Science	109	191	91	97	488
Teachers--English	127	201	62	110	500
Students--Science	1,042	1,294	532	586	3,454
Students--Reading Comprehension and Literature	1,007	1,294	539	606	3,446
Population IV					
Schools	26	39	21	29	115
Teachers--Science	105	144	39	100	388
Teachers--English	73	165	87	108	433
Students--Science	742	985	407	456	2,590
Students--Reading Comprehension and Literature	729	973	407	514	2,623
Stage 3					
Population II					
Schools--Civic Education	20	56	34	22	132
Schools--French[a]					195
Teachers--Civic Education	48	152	66	52	318
Teachers--French[a]					239
Students--Civic Education	461	1,372	844	555	3,232
Students--French Reading and Writing[a]					2,412
Students--French Reading and Listening[a]					2,010
Population IV					
Schools--Civic Education	22	54	32	16	124
Schools--French[a]					177
Teachers--Civic Education	51	148	59	27	285
Teachers--French[a]					224
Students--Civic Education	493	1,245	843	489	3,070
Students--French Reading and Writing[a]					1,819
Students--French Reading and Listening[a]					1,412

[a] No regional breakdown made.

1. *Northeast*: Connecticut, Delaware, Maine, Maryland, Massachusetts, New Hampshire, New Jersey, New York, Pennsylvania, Rhode Island, Vermont.
2. *North Central*: Illinois, Indiana, Iowa, Kansas, Michigan, Minnesota, Missouri, Nebraska, North Dakota, Ohio, South Dakota, West Virginia, Wisconsin,
3. *South*: Alabama, Arkansas, Florida, Georgia, Kentucky, Louisiana, Mississippi, North Carolina, Oklahoma,[1] Tennessee, Texas, Virginia, District of Columbia.
4. *West*: Alaska, Arizona, California, Colorado, Hawaii, Idaho, Montana, Nevada, New Mexico, Oklahoma, Texas, Utah, Washington, Wyoming, Oregon.

The figures reported in Table 19 are actual numbers of schools, teachers, and students involved in the data collection. The statistics reported in subsequent tables, however, are weighted on the basis of the original sampling plan. The sum of weights for statistics for the U.S. as a whole is equal in each case to the actual number of cases (excluding the rather small number of omissions). There is usually, however, some discrepancy between the actual number of units in a region and the sum of the weights for the units in the region because the weighting procedure was intended to represent best the results for the U.S. as a whole.

At Population I, all students were tested in science, reading comprehension, reading speed, and word knowledge, and completed the associated questionnaires. At Populations II and IV, two independent random samples were tested in each school in Stage 2. One sample took tests in science and word knowledge, and completed the associated questionnaires; the other sample took tests in reading comprehension, reading speed, literature, and word knowledge, and completed the associated questionnaires. Two samples of teachers at Populations II and IV were also involved in the data gathering. English teachers completed questionnaires dealing with the teaching of language and literature; science teachers completed questionnaires dealing with the teaching of science.

For the Stage 3 testing, two separate samples of schools were drawn at Population II and Population IV—one for civic education and one for French. In addition, a small *ad hoc* sample of ten schools was tested at Population I in French. Because this latter group cannot be

[1]Eastern counties of Oklahoma and Texas were classified as South; the western counties were classified as West. The classification scheme is the same one initially employed by the National Assessment Program.

considered as representative of any meaningful population, no analyses have been carried out for these schools.

Students at each population level responded to all instruments in the testing in civic education. In the French testing, it was necessary to divide the sample of schools at each population level randomly into two groups. One group of schools administered the tests of French reading and writing; the other group administered the French reading and listening tests. In the latter group, a small subsample (about four to six students per school) was administered the French speaking tests. The small samples for testing French speaking were necessitated by the fact that the tests had to be administered individually, required two tape recorders—one to present some of the stimulus material and one to record student responses—and were costly and time consuming to score. All students in the French testing at each population level completed the same questionnaires.

A total of 17,561 students in 522 schools were tested at the three population levels in Stage 2 (see Table 19). A total of 3,441 teachers completed the various questionnaires. According to the 1970 U.S. Census, the proportion of the population residing in the Northeast, North Central, South, and Western regions is 24%, 28%, 31%, and 17%, respectively. Regional figures are not readily available for the populations under study, however. If one assumes that these proportions are roughly comparable to those for the total population, the Northeast and North Central regions are overrepresented by about 6 percentage points and 9 percentage points, respectively; the South is underrepresented by about 15 percentage points. The figures for the West are comparable to the Census figures.

Table 19 also presents basic data on the schools, teachers, and students in the Stage 3 testing. The total number of students tested in Civic Education and French is 6,302 and 7,653 respectively. The regional breakdown of students for Civic Education at both population levels shows an overrepresentation of students in the North Central area and an underrepresentation of students from the Northeast and South. The percentage of students in the West accords with Census figures. Again, the assumption underlying these comparisons is that the proportions for the populations under study are roughly comparable to those for the total population.

No regional breakdowns have been made for the French data, both because French is not a required subject and because enrollments by region are not available. Furthermore, so many social and cultural factors lie behind the decision to study French as a foreign language that any conclusions would be extremely tenuous.

CHARACTERISTICS OF THE SCHOOLS

Information on a number of characteristics of the schools for each region at each population level is presented in Tables 20 through 25. Results for both Stage 2 (all subjects) and Stage 3 (Civic Education) are included for Populations II and IV. The results for the two stages are side by side; those for Stage 2 are presented first, and those for Stage 3 appear next in parentheses. For questionnaire items that had qualitative response categories, the proportion of responses in each category in each region is presented along with the proportion for the United States as a whole. These responses, it must be remembered, are weighted. For questionnaire items that required a numerical response on an interval scale, means and standard deviations are reported. The major exception to this general procedure is for items that required a numerical response but contained an open-ended category. For example, one item on the school questionnaire requested the principal to report the number of teacher aides employed in the school; the response categories were none, one, two, and three or more. In such cases, the full distribution is reported.

Tables 20, 21, and 22 present data oh the area served by the school, enrollment, size of faculty, and percent male teachers for Populations I, II, and IV, respectively. The item on the area served by the school had seven response categories: urban; suburban; rural; urban and suburban; urban and rural; suburban and rural; and urban, suburban, and rural. No definitions of urban, suburban, and rural were provided, but it seems reasonable to assume that school principals can make distinctions among the three. Interpretation of the results is complicated somewhat by the fact that four of the seven categories involve combined settings.

Schools in the South tend to have lower enrollments than schools in other regions at Population I, whereas at Population II schools in the North Central region are the smallest. At Population IV, the schools in the Northeast are somewhat smaller. In all regions at all population levels, school size is highly variable, but the proportions of boys and girls are not very disparate.

The data on faculty size must be viewed against enrollment data. Faculty size in all regions at Population I is considerably lower than for Populations II and IV. This, of course, reflects the smaller school size at Population I. Differences between regions at all population levels reflect differences in school size. For this reason, pupil-teacher ratios are reported. These ratios were obtained by dividing the average total school size by size of faculty. For the U.S. as a whole, the

Table 20

Selected Characteristics of Schools by Region for
Population I

Variable	Region				Total U.S.
	North-east	North Central	South	West	
Area Served by School					
% Urban	48	27	39	22	35
% Suburban	14	37	10	36	25
% Rural	11	8	3	10	9
% Urban/Suburban	11	8	24	9	12
% Urban/Rural	5	14	15	6	10
% Suburban/Rural	6	5	5	9	6
% Urban/Suburban/Rural	5	1	4	9	4
Enrollment					
Boys					
Mean	307	263	228	285	275
S.D.	138	125	89	121	126
Girls					
Mean	280	239	227	261	254
S.D.	132	104	94	101	114
Size of Faculty					
Mean	27.1	20.6	17.9	21.5	22.5
S.D.	13.1	12.2	6.8	8.0	11.8
Percent Male Teachers	14.5	11.4	9.5	15.3	12.8

pupil-teacher ratio was 23.5, 19.1, and 18.3 for Populations I, II, and IV, respectively, for Stage 2, and 19.4 and 18.9 for the latter two populations in Stage 3. At Population I, the pupil-teacher ratio ranges from 21.7 in the Northeast to 25.4 in both the South and West. At Population II the range is from 17.0 in the North Central at Stage 2 to 22.5 in the West at Stage 3; at Population IV the range is from 15.2 in the West at Stage 2 to 23.3 in the South at Stage 3. There appears to be no consistent pattern in pupil-teacher ratio as one moves from one population level to another within a region. The absence of any real patterns combined with the fact that the differences are rather small would lead one to conclude that there are no pronounced regional differences in pupil-teacher ratio.

Table 21

Selected Characteristics of Schools by Region for Population II

Variable	Region				Total U.S.
	Northeast	North Central	South	West	
Area Served by School					
% Urban	36 (11)	24 (18)	37 (32)	15 (21)	27 (21)
% Suburban	5 (16)	22 (6)	19 (10)	28 (13)	18 (9)
% Rural	17 (24)	17 (16)	0 (24)	21 (2)	15 (17)
% Urban/Suburban	18 (19)	12 (13)	32 (13)	7 (19)	16 (15)
% Urban/Rural	1 (3)	17 (24)	7 (12)	8 (39)	9 (21)
% Suburban/Rural	9 (16)	5 (24)	5 (4)	18 (7)	9 (15)
% Urban/Suburban/Rural	14 (11)	4 (0)	0 (4)	2 (0)	6 (3)
Enrollment					
Boys					
Mean	516 (454)	492 (467)	512 (427)	538 (453)	512 (453)
S.D.	286 (204)	337 (337)	281 (231)	302 (252)	307 (282)
Girls					
Mean	513 (423)	453 (444)	533 (418)	484 (409)	490 (429)
S.D.	273 (204)	244 (328)	310 (225)	274 (225)	272 (273)
Size of Faculty					
Mean	53.6 (48.1)	55.5 (50.0)	51.0 (40.8)	47.9 (38.3)	52.5 (45.5)
S.D.	24.5 (23.9)	39.4 (36.6)	26.3 (19.1)	24.3 (18.1)	30.6 (29.8)
Percent Male Teachers	49.5 (55.2)	48.0 (34.9)	35.9 (40.9)	56.7 (48.6)	48.3 (41.1)

Table 22

Selected Characteristics of Schools by Region for Population IV

Variable	Region				Total U.S.
	Northeast	North Central	South	West	
Area Served by School					
% Urban	7 (28)	14 (15)	42 (26)	14 (0)	16 (17)
% Suburban	14 (12)	11 (4)	20 (4)	15 (7)	14 (6)
% Rural	21 (23)	13 (21)	0 (24)	25 (4)	17 (20)
% Urban/Suburban	24 (4)	18 (11)	24 (11)	17 (35)	20 (13)
% Urban/Rural	2 (8)	27 (23)	9 (16)	14 (54)	15 (23)
% Suburban/Rural	18 (10)	0 (23)	2 (7)	11 (0)	8 (14)
% Urban/Suburban/Rural	14 (15)	16 (3)	4 (13)	4 (0)	11 (7)
Enrollment					
Boys					
Mean	510 (510)	634 (501)	637 (520)	610 (618)	597 (524)
S.D.	278 (260)	414 (334)	315 (272)	393 (469)	367 (332)
Girls					
Mean	495 (494)	637 (479)	671 (510)	578 (543)	590 (497)
S.D.	253 (304)	409 (336)	342 (275)	397 (338)	369 (313)
Size of Facility					
Mean	49.9 (59.1)	66.6 (50.4)	63.2 (58.9)	78.1 (49.7)	64.8 (53.9)
S.D.	20.6 (35.1)	40.7 (33.9)	27.5 (29.8)	121.2 (26.0)	69.4 (32.0)
Percent Male Teachers	51.5 (53.7)	53.5 (40.5)	40.7 (26.5)	63.5 (61.8)	53.7 (41.8)

The last school variable examined was the sex composition of the teaching staff. As was expected, females largely compose the teaching staff at Population I. The percent of males ranges from a low of 9.5% in the South to 15.3% in the West. At Population II, males are more in evidence, ranging from a low of 35.9% in the South to 56.7% in the West in Stage 2. At Population IV, males predominate in the Northeast, North Central, and West in both stages. Males are consistently underrepresented on the teaching staff of schools in the South at all population levels, however.

Tables 23 through 25 present data on the availability of ancillary personnel in the school. School librarians are the most widely reported ancillary personnel in all regions at all population levels, but they are not universally employed in schools. At Population I, 41% of the schools in the Northeast report not having a school librarian. At Populations II and IV, very few schools report not having a school librarian.

Guidance counselors are typically present in schools in all regions at Populations II and IV. 5% of the schools in the Northeast report not having guidance counselors at the latter level, however. At Population I, one-third of the students are in schools serviced by at least one guidance counselor. This figure appears to be high, and one wonders whether the respondents to this item were reacting to the guidance function that could be performed by the classroom teacher, or to a specially trained counselor.

School psychologists are not in great evidence at any population level. The percent of students in schools not served by a school psychologist is 69%, 77%, and 71% for Populations I, II, and IV, respectively, for the United States as a whole. The regional variations in school psychologists are rather notable. At Population I, 61% of the students in the North Central region are in schools where there is no school psychologist; the figure for the South is 81%. At Population II, from 58% to 91% of the students in the four regions are reported to be enrolled in schools that do not have a school psychologist; at Population IV, the range is from 62% to 94%. This latter figure is for the West; all schools in this region report having guidance counselors at this level. One can assume that at least some of the functions ordinarily performed by school psychologists are in fact carried out by guidance counselors.

The services of reading specialists appear to be available to over half the students in the United States at each population level. There are, however, some striking regional differences at Populations I and IV. In the former case, 26% of the students in the West are reported to be in schools in which a reading specialist is not available, compared to

Table 23

Personnel Services Provided by Schools for Each
Region at Population I (in percents)

	Region				Total U.S.
	Northeast	North Central	South	West	
Librarian					
None	41	40	18	30	35
1	57	51	82	63	59
2	1	6	0	5	3
3 or more	1	3	0	2	2
Guidance Counselor					
None	44	75	84	74	66
1	52	21	12	22	30
2	4	3	4	2	3
3 or more	0	1	0	2	1
School Psychologist					
None	74	61	81	66	69
1	25	39	19	32	30
2	1	0	0	0	0
3 or more	0	0	0	2	1
Reading Specialist					
None	35	47	54	26	41
1	45	45	42	64	47
2	18	8	4	6	10
3 or more	2	0	0	4	1
Teacher Aides					
None	38	48	42	20	39
1	3	18	32	24	17
2	18	17	6	18	16
3 or more	41	17	19	38	28
Social Worker					
None	83	61	78	89	75
1	15	39	20	11	24
2	0	0	2	0	0
3 or more	2	0	0	0	1
Science Lab Ass't. or Technician					
None	94	96	100	97	96
1	3	4	0	0	3
2	0	0	0	3	0
3 or more	3	0	0	0	1

Table 24

Personnel Services Provided by Schools for Each Region
at Population II (in percents)

	Region				Total U.S.
	Northeast	North Central	South	West	
Librarian					
None	7	0	3	3	3
1	72	70	57	71	69
2	18	18	40	10	20
3 or more	3	11	0	17	8
Guidance Counselor					
None	7	4	6	3	5
1	11	24	28	20	20
2	40	35	24	37	35
3 or more	42	38	42	40	41
School Psychologist					
None	73	58	91	73	71
1	27	37	9	25	27
2	0	5	0	3	2
Reading Specialist					
None	43	38	42	33	39
1	23	51	32	59	41
2	25	8	15	8	14
3 or more	9	3	11	0	5
Teacher Aide					
None	61	52	90	36	58
1	3	22	0	21	13
2	19	8	10	24	15
3 or more	15	19	0	18	14
Social Worker					
None	75	58	72	87	71
1	16	34	21	13	22
2	3	8	8	0	5
3 or more	5	0	0	0	1
Science Lab Ass't. or Technician					
None	56	89	100	71	78
1	41	7	0	17	17
2	3	0	0	10	3
3 or more	0	4	0	0	2

Table 25

Personnel Services Provided by Schools for Each Region
at Population IV (in percents)

	Region				Total U.S.
	Northeast	North Central	South	West	
Librarian					
None	5	0	0	0	1
1	79	52	40	57	59
2	13	34	52	26	29
3 or more	3	14	7	17	11
Guidance Counselor					
None	5	0	0	0	1
1	19	20	16	30	22
2	28	29	19	10	22
3 or more	49	51	65	60	55
School Psychologist					
None	76	62	82	94	77
1	24	38	13	6	23
2	0	0	0	0	0
3 or more	0	0	5	0	1
Reading Specialist					
None	64	32	56	39	46
1	36	65	35	55	50
2	0	3	9	6	4
Teacher Aides					
None	79	38	89	50	59
1	4	32	0	20	17
2	10	18	11	14	14
3 or more	6	13	0	17	10
Social Worker					
None	94	74	86	100	87
1	6	23	9	0	11
2	0	3	5	0	2
Science Lab Ass't. or Technician					
None	71	77	100	82	80
1	27	20	0	5	16
2	2	3	0	10	4
3 or more	0	0	0	3	1

54% for the South. At Population IV, 64% of the students in the Northeast are reported not to have such services available, contrasted with 32% in the North Central region.

Teacher aides appear to be used in the majority of schools at Population I but rather less frequently at Populations II and IV. Over one-half the students in all regions at Population I are in schools that utilize teacher aides but only the West at Population II and the North Central at Population IV report a majority of students being in schools that employ teacher aides. In general, the utilization pattern indicates that aides are used while students are acquiring basic skills and knowledge but not in the more advanced stages of learning.

Information on social workers and science laboratory assistants or technicians is also presented in Tables 23 through 25. Generally, social workers are not used in the schools except in the North Central area, and even here their use is limited. When social workers are employed in the school, other information suggests that they are used for some of the functions often performed by school psychologists. Thus, the somewhat lower incidence of school psychologists in the North Central region at all population levels may be explained by the relatively greater use of social workers.

The item on science laboratory assistants or technicians was included because of a special interest on the part of the international science committee. Science laboratory assistants or technicians are employed in the schools in a number of countries to prepare apparatus, assist in supervising laboratory work, etc. The data for the United States indicate hardly any use of such persons at Population I, and very limited use at Populations II and IV. The exceptions are the Northeast and West at Population II and the Northeast, North Central, and West at Population IV. These findings, however, must be interpreted with extreme care. No description of the role of science laboratory assistant or technician was provided and it is hard to judge how much the responses may have been affected by the respondents' unfamiliarity with the role. It is possible that advanced students might have been used in this capacity in some high schools and might accordingly have been reported as such.

CHARACTERISTICS OF TEACHERS AND TEACHING PRACTICES

Tables 26, 27, and 28 present data on characteristics of teachers and teaching practices. The sample of teachers included at Population I is defined somewhat differently from those at Populations II and IV. At

Population I, teachers were selected at random from the total list of classroom teachers in the participating schools. Thus, the teacher sample at Population I is representative of elementary school teachers, not merely of teachers of ten-year-olds. For Populations II and IV in the Stage 2 testing, a sample of teachers was selected from the list of science and English teachers in the participating schools. In Stage 3, a sample of the social studies teachers in each of the participating schools was chosen.

The data in Tables 26, 27, and 28 are typically reported in terms of the proportion of students exposed to teachers in various categories of the selected variables. This is because of the procedure followed in weighting the teachers. Means and standard deviations have not been computed even for such continuous variables as age and teaching experience, primarily because open-ended categories were employed, e.g., age 58 or older.

The data on age of teachers show no substantial differences between regions nor between population levels. In all cases except the South at Population I, over half the teachers report being 37 or younger; in the South, the figure is 41%.

Length of teaching experience is somewhat more variable. At Populations I and II, those reporting five or fewer years of teaching experience range from 54% to 68% in Stage 2, and from 24% to 43% in Stage 3. For the United States as a whole, the figures are 60% at both levels in Stage 2 and 37% for Population II in Stage 3. When the category of five to ten years is included, the figure rises to over 80%. At Population IV, however, the teaching cadre is somewhat more experienced. Overall, only 31% of the teachers have had five or fewer years of teaching experience in each Stage; another 26% report between five and ten years of teaching experience in Stage 2 and 18% in Stage 3. Regional differences within each population level are relatively small. Teachers at Population IV appear to be more highly experienced than teachers at either Populations I or II. One possible explanation for this is that the faculty at Populations I and II largely comprise females who teach for a few years before leaving to raise a family. Another possible explanation is that job transfers for husbands whose wives are teachers result in considerable turnover, which in turn results in a relatively inexperienced teaching staff at any point in time. This explanation seems quite plausible insofar as Population I is concerned. It is less tenable at Population II, where the percentage of male teachers is substantially greater. It may be that there is a tendency for junior high school teachers to move on to the senior high school level.

Data on the amount of time spent in planning lessons and in

Table 26

Selected Characteristics of Teachers and Teaching Practices
by Region for Population I (in percents)

Variable	Region				Total U.S.
	Northeast	North Central	South	West	
Age					
27 or younger	34	33	22	32	31
28-37	22	25	19	24	23
38-47	15	13	15	17	14
48-57	14	18	29	15	18
58 or older	15	12	16	12	13
Years of Teaching Experience					
Less than 5 years	56	63	54	68	60
5-10	28	17	20	17	21
11-20	10	17	17	13	14
21 or more years	5	4	9	2	5
Time Spent Each Week in Planning					
Less than 3 hours	7	8	5	11	8
Between 3 and 6 hours	55	41	46	41	46
Between 6 and 10 hours	23	36	30	31	30
More than 10 hours	16	14	19	14	15
Time Spent in Marking Papers					
Less than 3 hours	25	15	9	19	18
Between 3 and 6 hours	52	46	55	42	49
Between 6 and 10 hours	18	30	23	29	25
More than 10 hours	6	10	13	10	8
Membership in a General Teacher's Association					
Belonging	78	82	74	86	80
Membership in a Subject Matter Teaching Association					
Belonging	16	17	13	13	16
Determinants of What is Taught					
Teacher judgment of what students need to know					
Very important	73	79	89	74	78
Of some importance	23	21	10	25	21

Table 26--Continued

Variable	Region				Total U.S.
	Northeast	North Central	South	West	
Curriculum or Syllabus					
Very important	46	53	59	42	50
Of some importance	48	45	39	56	47
Prescribed textbook					
Very important	20	30	40	26	27
Of some importance	64	63	58	66	63
Standardized tests students will have to take					
Very important	7	10	15	9	10
Of some importance	64	61	68	54	62
What students will need to know for next grade or course					
Very important	64	68	84	68	69
Of some importance	32	31	16	30	29
Methods of Appraisal Standardized Tests					
Frequently	16	15	23	12	16
Occasionally	56	62	55	61	59
Teacher-made essay tests					
Frequently	26	19	39	17	24
Occasionally	43	47	32	44	43
Teacher-made objective tests					
Frequently	65	56	68	48	60
Occasionally	33	34	26	42	34
Performance on homework					
Frequently	51	39	53	31	44
Occasionally	33	35	32	38	34
Performance on projects, term papers, etc.					
Frequently	37	35	33	35	35
Occasionally	49	47	50	50	40
Within Class Grouping					
Always or almost always	17	20	35	19	21
Frequently	37	44	43	38	40
Occasionally	30	26	19	31	27
Rarely or never	16	10	4	12	11

Table 27

Selected Characteristics of Teachers and Teaching Practices
by Region for Population II (in percents)

Variable	Region				Total U.S.
	Northeast	North Central	South	West	
Age					
27 or younger	36	30	45	31	34 (37)
28-37	28	32	21	32	29 (25)
38-47	19	21	17	19	19 (23)
48-57	10	7	10	12	10 (16)
58 or older	8	10	7	6	8
Years of Teaching Experience					
Less than 5 years	55 (24)	58 (37)	68 (43)	63 (35)	60 (37)
5-10	22 (33)	25 (22)	16 (33)	22 (16)	22 (25)
11-20	16 (41)	12 (21)	14 (10)	11 (34)	13 (23)
21 or more years	7 (2)	5 (21)	3 (13)	4 (16)	5 (16)
Time Spent Each Week in Planning					
Less than 3 hours	9 (4)	6 (7)	3 (10)	8 (4)	7 (7)
Between 3 and 6 hours	33 (27)	35 (27)	41 (31)	41 (15)	37 (26)
Between 6 and 10 hours	35 (30)	31 (45)	41 (44)	35 (52)	34 (44)
More than 10 hours	23 (29)	27 (21)	15 (14)	16 (30)	22 (23)
Time Spent in Marking Papers					
Less than 3 hours	13 (16)	17 (18)	7 (8)	15 (10)	14 (14)
Between 3 and 6 hours	51 (54)	46 (41)	53 (64)	51 (47)	49 (50)
Between 6 and 10 hours	24 (24)	26 (29)	34 (18)	24 (35)	26 (26)
More than 10 hours	12 (5)	11 (13)	6 (9)	10 (9)	10 (11)
Membership in a General Teacher's Association					
Belonging	77	79	66	84	77
Membership in a Subject Matter Teaching Association					
Belonging	49	55	45	39	48

Table 27 Continued

Variable	Northeast	North Central	South	West	Total U.S.
Determinants of What is Taught					
Teacher judgment of what students need to know					
Very important	85	73	86	69	77
Of some importance	14	27	13	31	22
Curriculum or Syllabus					
Very important	35	30	42	17	31
Of some importance	60	65	51	64	61
Prescribed textbook					
Very important	18	20	31	12	19
Of some importance	66	56	58	52	58
Standardized tests students will have to take					
Very important	14	8	14	5	10
Of some importance	57	48	52	41	50
What students will need to know for next grade or course					
Very important	61	48	66	41	53
Of some importance	35	47	33	57	44
Methods of Appraisal					
Standardized Tests					
Frequently	9	10	9	14	10
Occasionally	38	42	39	28	37
Teacher-made essay tests					
Frequently	48	31	32	29	36
Occasionally	33	45	54	49	44

Table 27 Continued

Variable	Region					Total U.S.
	Northeast		North Central		South	West	

Variable	Northeast	North Central	South	West	Total U.S.
Teacher-made objective tests					
Frequently	70	66	80	57	67
Occasionally	26	30	18	31	27
Performance on homework					
Frequently	53	51	58	38	50
Occasionally	34	39	30	41	37
Performance on projects, term papers, etc.					
Frequently	36	34	38	45	38
Occasionally	57	56	56	45	54
Within Class Grouping					
Always or almost always	2 (0)	2 (2)	5 (1)	11 (0)	5 (1)
Frequently	16 (7)	9 (11)	16 (12)	12 (9)	13 (10)
Occasionally	37 (43)	35 (24)	34 (23)	37 (40)	36 (29)
Rarely or never	44 (50)	54 (63)	45 (64)	40 (51)	47 (60)

Table 28

Selected Characteristics of Teachers and Teaching Practices by Region
for Population IV (in percents)

Variable	Region				Total U.S.
	Northeast	North Central	South	West	
Age					
27 or younger	32	25	35	30	30
28-37	29	30	18	35	29
38-47	16	15	19	20	17
48-57	9	21	12	12	14
58 or older	15	9	16	3	11
Years of Teaching Experience					
Less than 5 years	28 (7)	29 (39)	30 (39)	38 (14)	31 (31)
5-10	30 (32)	24 (17)	18 (12)	26 (17)	26 (18)
11-20	18 (35)	25 (28)	30 (27)	27 (37)	24 (30)
21 or more years	24 (26)	22 (16)	23 (22)	10 (32)	20 (32)
Time Spent Each Week in Planning					
Less than 3 hours	8 (6)	5 (2)	8 (3)	4 (2)	6 (3)
Between 3 and 6 hours	40 (35)	26 (27)	32 (37)	46 (43)	36 (33)
Between 6 and 10 hours	34 (30)	36 (42)	35 (27)	27 (44)	33 (37)
More than 10 hours	18 (30)	33 (29)	25 (33)	23 (12)	24 (28)
Time Spent in Marking Papers					
Less than 3 hours	18 (3)	9 (7)	6 (6)	17 (2)	14 (5)
Between 3 and 6 hours	40 (72)	43 (50)	38 (49)	40 (55)	41 (54)
Between 6 and 10 hours	28 (11)	37 (34)	38 (34)	29 (20)	32 (29)
More than 10 hours	13 (14)	12 (9)	18 (10)	13 (23)	14 (12)
Membership in a General Teacher's Association					
Belonging	70	88	78	79	79
Membership in a Subject Matter Teaching Association					
Belonging	43	63	64	50	53

Table 28 Continued

Variable	Region				Total U.S.
	Northeast	North Central	South	West	
Determinants of What is Taught					
Teacher judgment of what students need to know					
Very important	75	80	85	77	78
Of some importance	24	20	15	21	21
Curriculum or Syllabus					
Very important	37	28	38	21	30
Of some importance	50	67	59	55	58
Prescribed textbook					
Very important	24	17	24	12	19
Of some importance	60	70	67	63	65
Standardized tests students will have to take					
Very important	17	4	17	4	10
Of some importance	52	51	60	51	52
What students will need to know for next grade or course					
Very important	47	48	67	42	48
Of some importance	46	48	31	53	47
Methods of Appraisal					
Standardized Tests					
Frequently	17	12	8	11	13
Occasionally	37	37	46	30	36
Teacher-made essay tests					
Frequently	45	52	46	51	49
Occasionally	28	36	43	37	35

Table 28 Continued

Variable	Region				Total U.S.
	Northeast	North Central	South	West	
Teacher-made objective tests					
Frequently	68	58	71	49	60
Occasionally	26	33	25	39	31
Performance on homework					
Frequently	44	50	52	38	45
Occasionally	40	39	37	50	42
Performance on projects, term papers, etc.					
Frequently	19	34	42	37	31
Occasionally	65	57	54	47	57
Within Class Grouping					
Always or almost always	1 (5)	3 (0)	7 (0)	1 (1)	2 (1)
Frequently	9 (2)	8 (8)	12 (8)	10 (14)	9 (8)
Occasionally	26 (28)	29 (22)	35 (38)	30 (46)	29 (31)
Rarely or never	64 (65)	59 (70)	47 (54)	59 (39)	59 (60)

marking papers were obtained from teachers. Such data must be interpreted with extreme care since they are self-reported estimates. Whether the teachers are supplying estimates of time spent on these duties over the week or two previous to answering the questionnaire or are reporting an average for the school year cannot be determined. If the former is true, then the reports might be serious underestimates because the data were gathered during April and May; figures for this time of the school year may differ considerably from those for the beginning or middle of the school year. At Population I, about 75% of the teachers in all regions report spending between three and ten hours a week in planning. The differences between regions are negligible. At Population II there is somewhat more variability. Substantially greater percentages of teachers in the Northeast and North Central regions report spending more than ten hours a week in planning than do teachers in the South and West in Stage 2. In Stage 3, teachers in the West report a substantial amount of time spent in preparation of lessons. There is also substantial variability at Population IV. The percentage of teachers in the Northeast who report spending more than ten hours a week in planning is considerably less than in the North Central (18% vs. 33%) in Stage 2. In Stage 3, teachers in the West appear to spend substantially less time in planning.

There are interesting differences among regions and among populations in the time spent marking papers. At Population I, 25% of the teachers in the Northeast report spending less than three hours a week marking papers, compared with 9% for the South. The proportions reporting spending between three and ten hours a week, however, do not differ markedly among regions, averaging 74%. At Population II, a substantially smaller percentage of the teachers in the South than elsewhere report spending three hours a week or less marking papers; in the other regions, the figure is between 13% and 17%. The great majority of teachers in both Stages (between 70% and 87%) report spending between three and ten hours a week on such tasks. At Population IV, the pattern is much the same, with the notable exception that a greater proportion (18%) of the teachers in the South in Stage 2 report spending more than ten hours a week marking papers than in the other three regions, and in Stage 3, 23% of the teachers in the West report spending more than ten hours a week in such activities.

Information about membership in professional associations was also obtained from all participating teachers. About 80% of the teachers reported belonging to a general teachers association or a teachers union. Differences among regions and among population levels were generally negligible. In contrast, there were considerable differences in responses to the items about membership in subject-matter teaching associations. At Population I, fewer than 20% of the teachers reported belonging to such associations. The differences among regions were negligible. At Populations II and IV, membership in subject-matter teaching associations was more widespread. Overall, 48% of the teachers at Population IV reported belonging to such associations. There was also substantial regional variability. At Population II, 39% of teachers in the West reported membership in such associations; for the other regions, the range was from 45% to 55%. At Population IV, 43% of the teachers in the Northeast reported belonging to a subject-matter teaching association; the figures for the other regions ranged from 50% to 64%. The overall results are fairly easily explained. Specialization increases as one moves from the elementary to the secondary school; this is accompanied by an increase in membership in subject-matter teaching associations. Interestingly, there is no corresponding decline in membership in general teachers associations or unions. This may be because of the role such groups play in negotiating salary and working conditions. The aberrant results for the West at Population II and for the Northeast at Population IV, however, cannot be explained.

A series of items was presented to ascertain teachers' judgments about the importance of various determinants on what they taught their students. The items were as follows:

What I think the students in my class will need when they leave school
A. Very important
B. Of some importance
C. Of little importance

The curriculum or syllabus
A. Very important
B. Of some importance
C. Of little importance

Prescribed textbook
A. Very important
B. Of some importance
C. Of little importance

Standardized tests that the student will have to take
A. Very important
B. Of some importance
C. Of little importance

What the students will need at the next grade or in their next course
A. Very important
B. Of some importance
C. Of little importance

The Stage 2 results for all regions at all populations are rather consistent. Teachers' own judgment of what the students need to know is ranked "very important" by a greater percentage of teachers in all regions at all populations than any other factor. The next most popular item that is ranked "very important" is "what the students will need at the next grade or in their next course." Again, the results are fairly consistent across regions and populations. The third most important determinant is the curriculum or syllabus, although the percentage of teachers regarding this as "very important" declines from Population I to Population IV. Interestingly, the use of standardized tests is rated "very important" by a smaller percentage of teachers in all regions at all populations than are any of the other determinants.

Factors that involve the teacher's own judgment are endorsed by a considerably greater percentage of teachers than are those that lie outside the teacher's control. Whether this is the reality of the situation or whether it simply reflects the teacher's belief that he or she controls what is taught cannot, of course, be known. In any case, the generally low status that teachers accord standardized tests in determining what is taught in the classroom is interesting in its own right. It leads one to wonder whether the influence of standardized testing on classroom teaching and learning is as noxious as some would have us believe.

Another set of items on the teacher questionnaire was intended to ascertain the relative frequency with which various types of appraisal were used by teachers in judging their students' work. The items were as follows:

Standardized tests
A. Frequently
B. Occasionally
C. Rarely or never

Teacher-made essay tests
A. Frequently
B. Occasionally
C. Rarely or never

Teacher-made objective tests
A. Frequently
B. Occasionally
C. Rarely or never

Performance on projects, term papers, etc.
A. Frequently
B. Occasionally
C. Rarely or never
Performance on homework
A. Frequently
B. Occasionally
C. Rarely or never

The most frequently-used method of appraisal in all regions at all populations is teacher-made objective tests. The proportion of teachers reporting that they use such tests frequently ranges from 48% in the West at Population I to 80% in the South at Population II. Typically, between one-half and two-thirds of the teachers report employing such tests frequently. The second most popular method of appraisal in all regions at Populations I and II is performance on homework. At Population IV, however, performance on homework and teacher-made essay tests are about equally popular. Teacher-made essay tests are used rather extensively at Population II, but relatively little at Population I. Regional differences are not particularly noteworthy.

The last item reported in Tables 26, 27, and 28 deals with the extent of within-class grouping procedures used by teachers. Differences among regions within each population are negligible. The differences among population levels are striking, however. At Population I, 61% of the teachers report that they frequently or almost always group students within the classroom for instructional purposes, e.g., reading groups, etc. At Population II, 18% report such use of within-class grouping in Stage 2 and 11% in Stage 3. At Population IV, the figures are 11% in Stage 2 and 9% in Stage 3. The difference between Populations II and IV is not appreciable, but the difference between Population I and the other populations is dramatic. This is readily understandable. At the elementary school level, a high value is placed on dividing the total class into smaller groups for instructional purposes. This is almost invariably true in the primary grades and is often maintained in grades four through six. At the secondary level, however, the picture is quite different. Grouping, if it is done at all, is usually undertaken to establish class groups. The teacher is presented with a group of students at a particular level of ability or proficiency and, presumably, with a restricted range. Sometimes such groups are established by school authorities, although they sometimes occur because of the nature of students who have elected a particular course. In any case, teachers often regard entering students as being somewhat homogeneous in ability, proficiency, or interest—whether they are or not. Accordingly, instruction is typically given to the class as a whole.

CHARACTERISTICS OF STUDENTS

Information on a number of student background characteristics is given in Tables 29, 30, and 31 for Populations I, II, and IV, respectively.

Table 29

Selected Personal and Background Characteristics
of Students by Region at Population I

Variable	Region				Total U.S.
	Northeast	North Central	South	West	
Sex of students (percent)					
Female	50	50	47	47	49
Age of Students (in months)					
Mean	128.9	126.7	126.4	126.9	127.4
S.D.	5.5	4.0	4.0	3.9	4.7
Father's Occupation (percent)					
Professional and Managerial	22	29	18	30	25
Clerical and Sales	11	14	12	9	12
Skilled	25	25	23	25	24
Semi-skilled and unskilled	19	17	18	18	18
Unclassifiable and unknown	24	14	29	20	21
Family Size (percent)					
Only children	5	3	6	2	4
One sibling	21	17	21	20	20
Two siblings	23	24	20	24	23
Three siblings	18	22	19	23	20
Four or more siblings	32	35	34	32	33
No. of Books in Home (percent)					
Fewer than 10 books	8	7	12	8	9
11-25 books	11	9	14	8	10
26-50 books	19	18	15	16	17
51 or more books	62	66	59	68	64
Hours spent reading for pleasure each week					
Mean	1.8	1.8	1.8	1.8	1.8
S.D.	1.4	1.3	1.4	1.4	1.4
Time spent watching TV per school day					
Mean	3.7	3.7	3.8	3.4	3.7
S.D.	2.2	2.0	2.3	2.1	2.1
Hours of homework each week					
Mean	4.7	4.2	5.9	3.3	4.5
S.D.	6.0	5.0	6.3	4.9	5.7

There is an almost even split between males and females in all regions at all population levels in both Stages. The sole exceptions are in the West at Populations II and IV in Stage 3, where 58% and 57%, respectively, of the students are males. Age data indicate that the overwhelming majority of students at Populations I and II in both Stages met the age criterion for inclusion in the study, i.e., Population I was to comprise students between ages 10.0 and 11.0, and Population II was to comprise students between ages 14.0 and 15.0. The standard deviations for the Northeast at these two levels in Stage 2 indicate that there was some minor violation of the target population definition. Reports from the field revealed that some school districts were not able to carry out the testing at the specified time but had to delay it because of particular local circumstances. This resulted in a somewhat higher standard deviation for age. It is unlikely that the results of the testing were appreciably affected, however. In Stage 3, the departure from the targeted testing date was somewhat more extreme, with the result that the average age was just under 15.0 in all regions. Again, it is unlikely that this influenced the test results substantially.

Information on father's occupation was coded using a slightly modified version of the *Dictionary of Occupational Titles* (U.S. Department of Labor, 1965). Despite attempts to secure as much detailed information as possible about the student's father's occupation, the proportion of unclassifiable or unknown responses was rather high—21% of the students at Population I alone. The great bulk of these cases simply did not provide enough detailed information to permit a classification.

There is a fairly substantial amount of variability of occupations in all regions at all population levels. The proportion of students reporting that their fathers hold professional and managerial positions increases from Population I to IV. This reflects the fact that about 25% of those in an age cohort drop out of school before graduation, and such students tend to come from homes where the father is employed below the professional/managerial level. Although the data for Population IV do indicate a certain amount of social bias when contrasted with Populations I and II, where schooling is compulsory, the extent of social bias in the United States is quite small in comparison with almost every other country that participated in the IEA studies.

There is relatively little variation among regions or among populations in family size and number of books in the home. Interestingly, about one-third of the students in each region at each population level in Stage 2 report having four or more siblings. About two-thirds of the students report that they have more than 50 books in their homes.

Table 30

Selected Personal and Background Characteristics
of Students by Region at Population II

Variable	Region				
	Northeast	North Central	South	West	Total U.S.
Sex of students					
% Female	53 (50)	53 (51)	54 (50)	52 (58)	53 (52)
Age of Students (in months)					
Mean	175.6 (178.3)	175.5 (179.2)	174.9 (178.9)	175.5 (179.5)	175.4 (179.1)
S.D.	5.2 (4.0)	3.8 (4.5)	3.9 (4.4)	3.8 (4.9)	4.3 (4.5)
Father's Occupation (percent)					
Professional and Managerial	29 (41)	34 (33)	32 (37)	36 (32)	32 (36)
Clerical and Sales	12 (9)	10 (8)	10 (10)	9 (13)	10 (10)
Skilled	30 (32)	29 (43)	25 (36)	26 (25)	28 (37)
Semi-skilled and unskilled	17 (11)	17 (9)	15 (10)	19 (11)	17 (10)
Unclassifiable and unknown	14 (7)	10 (7)	18 (8)	11 (9)	12 (8)
Family size (percent)					
Only child	5	3	5	2	4
One sibling	20	16	18	16	17
Two siblings	23	21	22	25	23
Three siblings	20	20	21	23	21
Four or more siblings	32	40	35	34	35
No. of Books in Home (percent)					
Fewer than 10 books	4 (2)	5 (5)	6 (6)	4 (3)	4 (5)
11-25 books	9 (5)	7 (6)	12 (10)	7 (7)	8 (7)
26-50 books	17 (14)	18 (17)	21 (18)	17 (13)	18 (16)
51 or more books	70 (79)	71 (72)	62 (66)	71 (78)	69 (72)
Hours spent reading for pleasure each week					
Mean	2.1 (2.1)	2.1 (2.0)	2.0 (2.0)	2.1 (2.2)	2.1 (2.0)
S.D.	1.5 (1.4)	1.5 (1.4)	1.5 (1.4)	1.5 (1.4)	1.5 (1.4)

Table 30 Continued

Variable	Region				Total U.S.
	Northeast	North Central	South	West	
Time spent watching TV each week					
Mean	15.6 (16.2)	15.2 (15.8)	15.7 (15.0)	15.7 (14.6)	15.5 (15.4)
S.D.	7.9 (7.9)	7.9 (8.0)	8.1 (7.4)	8.3 (8.8)	8.0 (7.4)
Hours of homework each week					
Mean	6.0 (6.4)	5.9 (5.4)	6.1 (5.2)	4.6 (6.0)	5.7 (5.6)
S.D.	5.2 (5.1)	4.9 (5.3)	5.5 (4.9)	4.1 (6.0)	5.0 (5.4)
Father's education (percent)					
Less than 5 years	4 (2)	4 (3)	6 (9)	5 (7)	5 (5)
Between 5 and 10 years	23 (19)	23 (26)	26 (23)	23 (19)	24 (23)
Between 10 and 15 years	56 (49)	50 (51)	46 (45)	46 (51)	51 (49)
More than 15 years	17 (31)	23 (19)	22 (23)	25 (23)	21 (22)
Mother's education					
Less than 5 years	4 (2)	3 (3)	5 (6)	6 (7)	5 (4)
Between 5 and 10 years	20 (15)	17 (23)	23 (21)	15 (18)	18 (20)
Between 10 and 15 years	65 (65)	65 (63)	59 (61)	62 (63)	63 (63)
More than 15 years	12 (18)	14 (11)	13 (13)	17 (12)	14 (12)

Table 31

Selected Personal and Background Characteristics
of Students by Region at Population IV

Variable	Region				Total U.S.
	Northeast	North Central	South	West	
Sex of students					
% Female	49 (55)	53 (50)	51 (50)	47 (57)	50 (52)
Age of Students (in months)					
Mean	208.7 (208.9)	209.9 (210.5)	210.6 (209.3)	210.6 (210.3)	209.7 (209.9)
S.D.	6.9 (6.1)	6.0 (5.6)	7.2 (7.2)	6.7 (6.2)	6.7 (6.3)
Father's Occupation (percent)					
Professional and Managerial	39 (45)	36 (40)	32 (39)	37 (53)	37 (43)
Clerical and Sales	9 (12)	12 (9)	9 (10)	8 (10)	10 (10)
Skilled	30 (28)	27 (38)	28 (33)	29 (22)	29 (33)
Semi-skilled and unskilled	13 (10)	17 (7)	16 (10)	15 (9)	15 (9)
Unclassifiable and unknown	8 (6)	7 (7)	16 (8)	12 (6)	10 (6)
Family size (percent)					
Only children	6	3	7	4	5
One sibling	23	16	20	13	19
Two siblings	26	23	21	24	24
Three siblings	18	22	17	22	20
Four or more siblings	27	36	35	32	32
No. of Books in Home (percent)					
Fewer than 10 books	4 (2)	5 (5)	5 (6)	4 (4)	5 (5)
11-25 books	7 (3)	10 (9)	12 (12)	11 (7)	9 (9)
26-50 books	17 (16)	20 (19)	23 (21)	17 (15)	19 (18)
51 or more books	71 (79)	65 (66)	60 (61)	68 (74)	67 (68)
Hours spent reading for pleasure each week					
Mean	2.1 (2.2)	1.9 (2.0)	2.1 (2.0)	2.0 (2.2)	2.0 (2.1)
S.D.	1.3 (1.4)	1.3 (1.4)	1.3 (1.4)	1.3 (1.4)	1.3 (1.4)

Table 31 Continued

Variable	Region				Total U.S.
	Northeast	North Central	South	West	
Time spent watching TV each week					
Mean	13.1 (12.1)	12.8 (13.1)	13.9 (12.2)	12.6 (11.0)	13.0 (12.2)
S.D.	7.9 (8.2)	7.9 (8.1)	8.0 (8.3)	8.2 (7.4)	8.0 (8.2)
Hours of homework each week					
Mean	6.8 (6.1)	6.0 (5.0)	6.0 (5.2)	4.8 (5.6)	6.0 (5.4)
S.D.	5.6 (5.6)	5.1 (4.6)	4.9 (4.9)	4.4 (5.4)	5.1 (5.0)
Father's education (percent)					
Less than 5 years	3 (3)	5 (4)	5 (9)	7 (3)	5 (5)
Between 5 and 10 years	24 (14)	26 (28)	31 (26)	22 (20)	25 (24)
Between 10 and 15 years	56 (56)	54 (52)	51 (44)	53 (50)	54 (50)
More than 15 years	18 (27)	15 (16)	13 (21)	18 (26)	17 (20)
Mother's education (percent)					
Less than 5 years	3 (4)	4 (3)	4 (5)	8 (6)	4 (4)
Between 5 and 10 years	19 (13)	19 (21)	25 (24)	18 (15)	19 (20)
Between 10 and 15 years	68 (66)	66 (67)	64 (59)	66 (67)	67 (65)
More than 15 years	11 (17)	11 (9)	7 (13)	7 (13)	10 (12)

At all population levels in both Stages, the regional variations in reading patterns and time spent watching television are negligible. At Population I, students report watching television an average of 3.7 hours a day on *school* days. In contrast, students report spending an average of 1.8 hours per *week* reading for pleasure. That is, students report spending twice as much time watching television each school day as they spend reading for pleasure in a week. At Populations II and IV, the item on time spent watching television included listening to the radio and was phrased somewhat differently. At these levels, students were asked to report the amount of time spent in these activities on a weekly basis. At Population II, students report spending an average of 15.5 and 15.4 hours a week watching television or listening to the radio in Stages 2 and 3, respectively. In contrast, the same students report spending an average of 2.1 and 2.0 hours a week reading for pleasure in Stages 2 and 3, respectively. Thus, for every hour spent in reading for pleasure, about 7 1/2 hours are spent watching television or listening to the radio. The results for Population IV are quite similar. Students report spending an average of 13.0 and 12.2 hours a week watching television or listening to the radio in Stages 2 and 3, respectively, and 2.0 and 2.1 hours reading for pleasure. Thus, for every hour spent in reading for pleasure about 6½ hours are spent watching television or listening to the radio. Interestingly, time reported spent in reading for pleasure is highly stable across population levels, about two hours a week, whereas television viewing shows a systematic decline from over 18 hours a week at Population I to between 12 and 13 hours a week at Population IV for the two Stages.

Data on the number of hours of homework in all subjects each week offer another contrast to time spent watching television and listening to the radio.[2] At Population I, students report spending an average of 4.5 hours a week doing homework. The range is from 3.3 hours in the West to 5.9 hours in the South. In contrast, students report spending, on average, 3.7 hours watching television each *school* day. At Population II, students report spending an average of 5.7 and 5.6 hours a week doing homework in Stages 2 and 3, respectively, with a range of from 4.6 in the West in Stage 2 to 6.4 in the Northeast in Stage 3. This is in contrast to the average of about 15 1/2 hours a week spent watching television and listening to the radio. At Population IV, students report spending an average of 6.0 and 5.4 hours a week doing homework in Stages 2 and 3, respectively, compared with 13.0 and 12.2 hours a week watching television or listening to the radio in the

---

[2]It is possible that some students do their homework while listening to the radio or watching television, which makes it difficult to consider separately the amount of time spent on such activity.

two Stages. The difference among regions in time spent doing homework is again substantial, ranging from 4.8 hours in the West to 6.8 hours in the Northeast in Stage 2. The differences among population levels in time spent on homework is not large. Students at Population I report doing the least amount of homework each week (4.5 hours), whereas students at Population IV in Stage 2 report doing the most (6.0 hours). In Stage 3, Population II students report an average of 5.6 hours of homework a week, compared with 5.4 hours at Population IV. This slight decrease in the Stage 3 results is puzzling. The average difference of about one to 1½ hours between students who are predominantly fifth graders and students who are in twelfth grade seems somewhat small. It may be that there is systematic overclaiming among the Population I students.

Background information is also presented on reported amount of father's and mother's education for Populations II and IV. (These questions were not asked at Population I since a pilot study indicated that ten-year-olds could not furnish valid information.) Tables 30 and 31 show relatively little variation among regions and Stages for each variable at each population level. It is difficult, however, to say much about these data. The response categories were specified internationally and do not accord well with U.S. schooling patterns. For example, it is not possible to state what proportion of the fathers or mothers of students in the U.S. sample completed high school. This is one of the drawbacks of a study in which the U.S. was but one of a large number of countries.

ACHIEVEMENT TEST PERFORMANCE OF STUDENTS

The various achievement test scores described below, with the exception of the scores obtained from the Reading Speed Tests, have been corrected for guessing. In the case of the Reading Speed Test, two scores are presented. The first, Item Reached, denotes the last item marked by the student on a very simple 40-item test; this is an indication of how fast the individual reads because the test was timed (four minutes was allotted for the task). The second score, Error Count, is a count of the number of items answered incorrectly on the first page of the test, which contained nine items. Since the same Reading Speed Test was used at both Populations I and II, the scores between populations are directly comparable.

The results for Population I are presented in Table 32. The highest means on the Science Test were obtained in the North Central and West. The mean for the Northeast is slightly lower, and the mean for

Table 32

Total Achievement Test Performance of Students by Region
at Population I

Variable	Region				Total
	Northeast	North Central	South	West	
Science test					
Mean	17.1	19.4	14.2	19.2	17.7
S.D.	9.2	8.8	9.5	8.7	9.2
Reading Comprehension Test					
Mean	16.6	18.3	12.9	18.1	16.8
S.D.	11.5	11.4	11.3	11.3	11.5
Reading Speed Test-- Item reached					
Mean	24.3	25.6	23.3	25.3	24.7
S.D.	8.8	8.2	8.9	8.2	8.6
Reading Speed Test-- Error count					
Mean	1.0	0.9	1.3	0.9	1.0
S.D.	1.5	1.5	1.7	1.5	1.5
Word Knowledge Test					
Mean	17.2	19.0	13.9	18.0	17.4
S.D.	11.5	10.7	11.3	10.5	11.2

the South is decidedly lower (0.38 standard deviation units lower than the mean for the U.S.). In Reading Comprehension, the pattern of results is quite similar to that in Science. The results for the two scores obtained from the Reading Speed Test, on the other hand, show very small regional variations, although the pattern of results is the same. The Word Knowledge Test results show the same regional pattern as those in Science and Reading Comprehension: the North Central and West have the highest means, the Northeast is slightly lower, and the South decidedly lower.

It is not easy to explain these results. Previous findings, especially those of the National Assessment of Educational Progress (NAEP) have shown generally lower results in the South. The somewhat lower results for the Northeast were somewhat unexpected, however, especially in light of the NAEP results. The Northeast's slightly lower performance may stem from the fact that more large city school systems are included in the sample from the Northeast than in the samples from other regions; the level of student performance in large city school districts tends to be lower than the performance of students in suburban and small town school districts. The lower performance of the students in the South, on the other hand, is consistent with the results of the NAEP as well as other studies in which regional comparisons have been made. The sole exception is on the Reading Speed Test, where the performance of students from the South is much closer to that of the other regions. One possible explanation might lie in the nature of the Reading Speed Test. The test consisted of a number of items that were extremely simple and the task for the student was to work through them as quickly as possible. The other tests, however, contained items of graduated difficulty.

Results for students at the Population II level are presented in Table 33. Again, the performance of students in the South on all tests except the Reading Speed Test is somewhat lower (about 0.2 standard deviations). In Reading Speed, the students in the South performed at about the same level as did students in all other regions. Outside the South, there was relatively little regional variation on the tests; no region performed clearly above the others in Stage 2. In Stage 3, students in the Northeast performed substantially higher than students in the North Central and the South and, to a lesser extent, than students in the West. Students in the North Central scored somewhat higher than students in other regions on the Reading Comprehension and Word Knowledge Tests in Stage 2 but were slightly below the U.S. mean in Stage 3. Students in the Northeast had the highest means on the Literature and Civic Education Tests, and the West outperformed all regions on the Science Test. The differences, outside the South, are not substantial.

The results for Population IV (see Table 34) require careful interpretation. As noted before, schooling is not compulsory at this age level. For the U.S. as a whole, 25% of an age group does not complete high school.[3] This does not mean, however, that 25% of an age group in each region does not complete high school. There is probably some regional variation in the high school dropout rate.

The somewhat lower performance of the South is immediately apparent. The means for the South range from about two-tenths to one-third of a standard deviation below the U.S. mean on each test. This is similar to the results obtained for Populations I and II, where schooling is compulsory. Again, variation among the other three regions is generally small and erratic.

The generally lower performance level of the South occurred on almost all the total scores on the tests at all population levels. To find out whether the same findings obtained for each topical area in each

<hr>

[3]Although this figure may seem high, it is quite low compared to most other countries. Among the IEA countries for instance, 93% of an age group does not complete high school in Germany or in Iran.

Table 33

Total Achievement Test Performance of Students
by Region at Population II

Stage and Variable	Region				Total
	Northeast	North Central	South	West	
Stage 2					
Science Test					
Mean	21.4	22.1	18.8	22.9	21.5
S.D.	10.9	11.8	11.9	11.6	11.6
Reading Comprehension Test					
Mean	27.1	28.7	24.6	27.1	27.3
S.D.	11.3	11.3	12.5	11.4	11.6
Literature Test					
Mean	17.2	16.9	14.9	16.0	16.5
S.D.	8.2	8.9	9.5	9.0	8.8
Reading Speed Test-- Item Reached					
Mean	32.0	33.1	32.3	32.1	32.4
S.D.	7.1	7.1	7.8	7.1	7.3
Reading Speed Test-- Error Count					
Mean	0.3	0.3	0.4	0.4	0.3
S.D.	0.8	0.7	0.8	1.0	0.8
Word Knowledge Test					
Mean	17.0	17.6	14.9	16.9	16.8
S.D.	8.6	8.9	9.2	8.5	8.8
Stage 3					
Civic Education Achievement Test					
Mean	28.1	24.3	22.9	26.5	24.6
S.D.	8.7	9.4	10.1	10.0	9.9
Word Knowledge Test					
Mean	19.7	15.7	14.6	18.2	16.3
S.D.	8.1	9.2	9.9	10.3	9.6
French Reading Test[a]					
Mean					7.6
S.D.					7.5
French Writing Test[a]					
Mean					46.6
S.D.					27.7
French Listening Test[a]					
Mean					6.1
S.D.					7.2
French Speaking Test[a]					
Mean					118.2
S.D.					45.0

[a] No regional analyses carried out.

Table 34

Total Achievement Test Performance of Students
by Region at Population IV

Stage and Variable	Region				Total
	Northeast	North Central	South	West	
Stage 2					
Science Test					
Mean	14.4	14.1	10.5	13.4	13.7
S.D.	9.5	9.6	8.8	9.4	9.5
Reading Comprehension Test					
Mean	21.4	22.5	18.7	22.7	21.7
S.D.	12.1	11.7	11.9	12.4	12.1
Literature Test					
Mean	22.1	21.9	20.1	22.6	21.9
S.D.	7.9	7.7	8.2	7.1	7.7
Word Knowledge Test					
Mean	14.4	13.9	11.3	13.6	13.7
S.D.	10.0	9.4	9.7	9.6	9.7
Stage 3					
Civic Education Achievement Test					
Mean	25.0	21.2	19.5	23.4	21.4
S.D.	8.3	8.7	9.4	9.5	9.7
Word Knowledge Test					
Mean	16.3	12.5	11.4	15.6	13.2
S.D.	9.8	9.5	9.7	10.0	9.9
French Reading Test[a]					
Mean					17.5
S.D.					9.5
French Writing Test[a]					
Mean					57.6
S.D.					27.3
French Listening Test[a]					
Mean					13.8
S.D.					11.5
French Speaking Test[a]					
Mean					187.6
S.D.					57.2

[a] No regional analyses carried out.

subject, it was necessary to examine performance on the various subtests of the achievement measures. In science, for example, there were enough items available in Earth Science, Biology, and Chemistry to obtain subscores in these areas at all population levels. In Physics, however, there were not enough items in the Population I test to obtain a meaningful subscore. Thus, the Physics subscore was obtained only for Populations II and IV. In Literature, two subscores were calculated, one for Literary Comprehension and one for Literary Interpretation. In Reading Comprehension, a number of subscores were obtained, but these were so highly correlated that separate consideration of them seemed unwarranted. No subscores were obtained in Civic Education because of the small numbers of items available to form the subscores.

A check on the similarity of the samples in Stages 2 and 3 for Populations II and IV can be made by comparing the Word Knowledge Test means across stages. This was the only test that was administered in both stages. The means for the United States at Population II were 16.8 and 16.3 for Stages 2 and 3, respectively. This is a negligible difference. Differences for regions between Stages 2 and 3 are generally larger. In the Northeast, students participating in the Stage 3 testing scored 2.7 points higher than their counterparts in Stage 2. The pattern, however, is rather inconsistent. Students in the Northeast and West in Stage 3 scored higher than their Stage 2 counterparts, whereas in the North Central the opposite was the case. It is quite likely that such differences are due to sampling fluctuations.

Table 35

Selected Achievement Test Subscores for Students
by Region at Population I

Subtest	No. of Items	Region				Total
		Northeast	North Central	South	West	
Earth Science	9					
Mean		4.8	5.2	4.0	5.0	4.8
S.D.		2.5	2.4	2.7	2.4	2.5
Biology	13					
Mean		5.0	5.8	4.1	5.7	5.3
S.D.		3.5	3.3	3.5	3.3	3.4
Physics	14					
Mean		6.2	7.2	5.2	7.2	6.5
S.D.		3.9	3.8	4.0	3.8	3.9

Table 36

Selected Achievement Test Subscores for Students
by Region at Population II

Subtest	No. of Items	Region				Total
		Northeast	North Central	South	West	
Biology	19					
Mean		6.2	6.4	5.6	6.4	6.2
S.D.		3.2	3.4	3.6	3.5	3.4
Chemistry	19					
Mean		3.7	3.7	3.1	3.9	3.7
S.D.		3.5	3.7	3.7	3.6	3.6
Physics	22					
Mean		8.2	9.5	7.3	8.7	8.2
Practical	20					
Mean		3.3	3.5	2.8	3.9	3.4
S.D.		3.3	3.4	3.3	3.5	3.4
Literature Comprehension	15					
Mean		8.1	7.8	6.9	7.5	7.7
S.D.		4.0	4.2	4.7	4.2	4.2
Literature Interpretation	21					
Mean		9.1	9.1	8.1	8.5	8.8
S.D.		4.9	5.3	5.4	5.4	5.2

At Population IV, the results are quite similar. The mean scores for the United States on the Word Knowledge Test are 13.7 and 13.2 for Stages 2 and 3, respectively. Again Stage 3 students in the Northeast and West performed somewhat higher than their Stage 2 counterparts, and students in the North Central performed somewhat lower. Students in the South in the two Stages performed at almost identical levels. Since the samples for the two stages can be viewed as replications and since the project encountered a fair degree of resistance in Stage 2 but not in Stage 3, the results of the Word Knowledge Tests would lead one to conclude that the lack of cooperation at Stage 2 probably did not result in the introduction of much bias.

Tables 35, 36, and 37 present subtest scores for Science and Literature for Populations I, II, and IV. The same findings that obtained for total test performance hold for subtest performance. That is, students in the South scored, on average, about one-fourth to one-third standard deviation below the mean for the United States on every subtest in Science and Literature at each population level.

Table 37

Selected Achievement Test Subscores for Students
by Region at Population IV

Subtest	No. of Items	Region				Total
		Northeast	North Central	South	West	
Biology	18					
Mean		6.3	6.1	5.3	6.1	6.1
S.D.		3.2	3.2	3.2	3.3	3.2
Chemistry	18					
Mean		2.1	2.3	1.3	2.2	2.1
S.D.		2.9	2.9	2.6	2.8	2.9
Physics	18					
Mean		3.4	3.2	1.9	2.8	3.1
S.D.		3.6	3.5	3.0	3.5	3.5
Practical	12					
Mean		2.6	2.6	2.0	2.5	2.5
S.D.		2.5	2.6	2.6	2.4	2.5
Literature Comprehension	15					
Mean		10.0	9.9	9.1	9.9	9.8
S.D.		3.6	3.7	4.0	3.3	3.6
Literature Interpretation	21					
Mean		12.1	12.1	11.1	12.6	12.1
S.D.		4.9	4.6	5.0	4.4	4.7

Performance in the other regions was quite similar; what differences exist are small and inconsequential. The sole exception is the North Central region at Population I. Students in this region scored about one-sixth of a standard deviation above the U.S. mean on the Earth Science, Biology, and Chemistry subtests.

Although regional differences in performance are informative, increases in performance in each subject area from Population I to Population IV are also interesting. Estimates of increases in performance were obtained for Science, Reading Comprehension, and Word Knowledge according to the following procedure. First, Population II was selected as the base population. Second, the anchor items (i.e., items common to tests in Populations I and II and items common to tests in Populations II and IV) were used to estimate the difference in performance from the Population II mean in terms of Population II standard deviation units for the U.S. as a whole. This was done by subtracting the Population II mean on the anchor items for each region

Table 38

Estimates of Increase in Science, Reading Comprehension, and Word Knowledge Test Performance from Population I to Population IV for Each Region of the United States

Subject and Regions	Level of Performance for Population I[a]	Level of Performance for Population IV[a]	Estimated Increase in Performance from Pop. I to Pop. IV
Science			
Northeast	-.88	.69	1.57
North Central	-.65	.69	1.34
South	-1.19	.26	1.45
West	-.69	.57	1.26
Reading Comprehension			
Northeast	-1.24	.65	1.89
North Central	-1.05	.68	1.73
South	-1.52	.41	1.93
West	-.95	.63	1.63
Word Knowledge			
Northeast	-1.25	.63	1.93
North Central	-1.17	.68	1.85
South	-1.53	.34	1.87
West	-1.25	.62	1.87

[a] Relative to United States mean and standard deviation for Population II.

from the Population I or IV mean for the same anchor items for each region and dividing the difference by the U.S. Population II standard deviation. Finally, the difference between the Population I and Population IV performance levels, expressed in terms of Population II performance, was obtained. This provides an estimate of the increase in performance from Population I to Population IV.

This approach to the estimation of increments in performance is somewhat hazardous due to the small number of anchor items included in the tests at adjoining levels. For example, in Science there are eleven items common to Populations I and II and twenty items common to Populations II and IV. Recognizing this limitation, however, estimates of increases in performance were obtained; they are presented in Table 38 and Figures 9, 10, and 11. Table 38 and Figure 9 present the results for Science for each of the four regions. The first column in Table 38 expresses the performance level of the average student in Population I in each region in relation to the mean of the U.S. at Population II as a zero point for each subject. Thus, the average Population I student in the South is −1.19 standard deviation units below the Population II Science mean, compared to the average Population I student in the North Central, who is only −0.65 units below the Population II Science mean. The second column expresses the performance level of the average student in Population IV in each region in relation to the Population II mean and standard deviation. The average Population IV student in the South is 0.26 standard deviation units above the Population II Science mean, compared to the average student in the Northeast and North Central, who are .69 standard deviation units above the Population II mean. The third column shows the estimated increase in performance from Population I to Population IV in terms of Population II standard deviation units. This was obtained by computing the difference between the figures in the first two columns.

The same information for Science is presented graphically in Figure 9. Here, the left end of each bar represents the average performance of Population I students in a region, the right end of the bar the average performance of Population IV students, and the length of the bar the increase in level of performance from Population I to IV.

The second and third sections of Table 38, and Figures 10 and 11, present the same information for Reading Comprehension and Word Knowledge. In all three tests, the South shows the lowest level of performance at Populations I and IV. The increase in performance from Populations I to IV shows a somewhat different picture. In Science, the range of increase is from 1.26 standard deviation units for the West to 1.57 units for the Northeast. The increase in performance

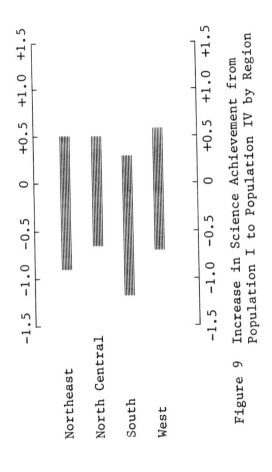

Figure 9   Increase in Science Achievement from
Population I to Population IV by Region

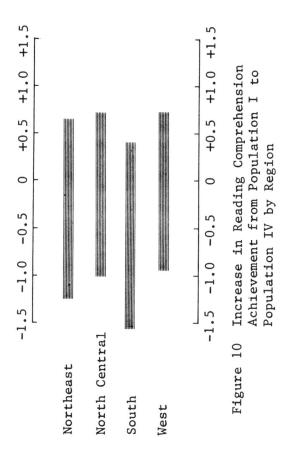

Figure 10   Increase in Reading Comprehension Achievement from Population I to Population IV by Region

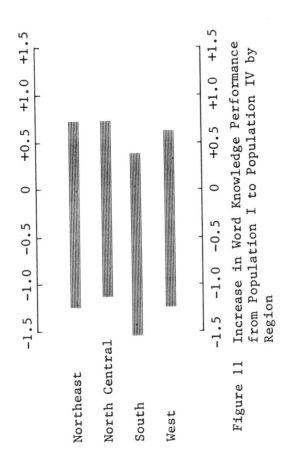

Figure 11   Increase in Word Knowledge Performance
from Population I to Population IV by
Region

for the South, 1.45 standard deviation units, is second only to the Northeast. In Reading Comprehension, the range of increase from Populations I to IV is from 1.63 standard deviation units for the West compared to 1.93 standard deviation units for the South; in Word Knowledge the range of increase from Populations I to IV is from 1.85 units for the North Central to 1.93 units for the Northeast.

In all cases except one—Science performance in the North Central region—the increase in performance from Populations I to II is substantially greater than the increase from Populations II to IV. Since about one-fourth of an age group in the U.S. leaves school between the Population II and Population IV levels, one would expect the more select student group at Population IV to register a higher increment over the Population II level than the Population II over the Population I group. The fact that just the opposite was found is rather puzzling. There is no apparent explanation for these findings.

In Stage 3, a slight modification of the procedure for estimating increments was used because only Populations II and IV were tested in Civic Education. No regional analyses were carried out in French, and only the Reading and Listening Comprehension Tests in this subject

Table 39

Estimates of Increase in Civic Education Achievement
Test Performance from Population II to IV for Each
Region of the United States, and for French Reading
and Listening Comprehension Test Performance for
the United States

Subject and Group	Estimated Increase from Population II to Population IV[a]
Civic Education	
Northeast	.74
North Central	.80
South	.76
West	.78
French Reading	2.11
French Listening Comprehension	1.89

[a] Relative to U.S. standard deviation for Population II.

contained anchor items that permitted a link between the two populations. The results of the estimation process are presented in Table 39. In Civic Education, the increments from Population II to IV are quite similar for all regions. Thus, the lower performance of students in the South at both levels is a function of the lower initial level of performance and not of a slower rate of growth. Similarly, the higher level of performance in the Northeast at both levels is a function of the initially higher level of performance. There is less to be said about French Reading and Listening Comprehension. There is a very large increment from Population II to IV on both tests. The growth, in fact, is at least as much as takes place between Populations I and IV for those subjects that were tested at all three population levels. Much of this increment, however, may be due to the very low initial level of performance at Population II. In French Reading, for example, the United States scored lowest among the six countries that tested at this level.

SUMMARY

This chapter has described differences among the four major regions of the United States. Characteristics of schools, teachers, and students in each of the four regions used by the National Assessment of Educational Progress were presented and discussed. Generally, differences were slight and no consistent pattern was evident. Test performance data, on the other hand, showed clear differences. In almost all subjects at all Population levels, students in the South performed substantially below students in the other three regions. There were small and inconsistent differences among the other three regions. Examination of the increases in performance from Population I to IV in Science, Reading Comprehension, and Word Knowledge, and from Population II to IV in Civic Education showed fairly similar amounts of increase in performance for all regions. Thus, the generally lower level of performance in the South is largely a function of an initially lower level of performance. The increase in performance in the South in each subject was quite comparable to that shown in the other regions.

Chapter 5

Differences Between Predominantly White and Predominantly Black Schools

When the current group of IEA studies was being planned, it was decided to obtain information on ethnic and racial composition of the schools in the United States sample. Up-to-date information about schools, teachers, and students in predominantly white and predominantly black schools could be useful in estimating the amount of progress made in extending equality of educational opportunity to all students. A set of questions was incorporated in the United States version of the School Questionnaire completed by each school principal to ascertain the proportion of Caucasian, black, Hispanic, and Oriental students in each school. Initially, we had also hoped to obtain racial and ethnic data for each participating student and teacher, but such intrusions on individual privacy were considered inappropriate.

The data were checked extremely carefully; if the data were found to be internally inconsistent or in conflict with other known information about the school, correspondence was initiated with school personnel to reconcile the matter.

The percentages of students in each racial or ethnic category were examined both to decide which groups contained sufficient cases for further analysis and to establish cutoff points. It was quickly determined that there were too few schools containing sizable proportions of Hispanic or Oriental students for any meaningful analysis. There were, however, enough schools containing large proportions of white or of black students. Inspection of the distributions led to the decision to limit analyses to schools in which *at least 90%* of the students were either white or black. This yielded the number of schools, teachers, and students shown in Table 40.[1] (Although the headings of each table

---

[1] The data in Table 40 are for Populations I and II only. The number of predominantly black schools in Population IV was so small as to make the results of analyses on those data questionable.

104

Table 40

Number of Schools, Teachers, and Students Classified
as White or Black at Populations I and II

| Group | Type of School | | Total U.S. |
	White[a]	Black[a]	
Population I			
Schools	185	21	262
Teachers	1,145	141	1,632
Students	3,472	433	5,448
Population II			
Stage 2			
Schools	93	9	145
Science Teachers	288	40	488
English Teachers	314	35	500
Science Students	1,990	206	3,454
English Students	1,985	211	3,446
Stage 3			
Schools	66	6	132
Teachers	163	6	320
Students	1,424	102	3,232

[a] The categories "white" and "black" refer to schools that have predominantly white or black student populations, i.e., 90% or more of the students in the school are white or black. Source of information is the school principal.

are "white" and "black," this does not mean that an *exclusively* white or black group is being described. On the contrary, it denotes a group of schools in which the student population is *predominantly* [i.e., at least 90%] white or black. No racial information is available about the faculty or administrators of the schools, nor is this essential to answering questions about the school conditions and resources being provided to students in racially different schools in the United States.)

Tables 41 and 42 present data on school location, enrollment, size and composition of faculty, and the availability of ancillary services. Stage 2 results are presented first; Stage 3 results are presented in parentheses. There are substantial differences in location between the white and the black schools. The black schools are located primarily in urban areas, whereas the white schools are located in a variety of settings, i.e., urban, suburban, rural, and various combinations of these. At both age levels, the black schools are appreciably larger than the white schools. The faculty is also considerably larger, however, and the student-teacher ratios are rather close. At Population I, the student-teacher ratio is 24.6 for the white schools and 25.5 for the black schools. At Population II, the ratios are 19.3 and 20.7 for the white and black schools, respectively, in Stage 2, and 17.8 and 20.7 in Stage 3. The sex composition of the faculty is rather similar at each age level but differs between age levels; this reflects the difference between elementary and secondary education.

Data on ancillary services indicate that the black schools have a somewhat higher level of ancillary services. The sole exception is the category of Teacher Aides at Population II. Here, the white schools

Table 41

Selected Characteristics of White and Black
Schools at Population I

Variable	Type of School		Total U.S.
	White	Black	
Location of Residence[a]			
Percent Urban	16	80	35
Percent Rural	17	10	9
Percent Urban and Suburban	9	10	12
Enrollment			
Average number of boys	242	307	275
Average number of girls	221	304	254
Average Size of Faculty	18.8	23.9	22.9
Percent Male Teachers	13.7	9.3	12.8
Personnel Services Provided			
Percent having Librarian	59	63	64
Percent having Guidance Counselor	22	50	34
Percent having School Psychologist	32	40	31
Percent having Reading Specialist	51	70	59
Percent having Teacher Aides	55	84	61

[a] Percentages do not add to 100% because of the omission of certain categories, e.g., suburban. There are substantial differences in residential location of students in predominantly white and predominantly black schools.

Table 42

Selected Characteristics of White and Black Schools
at Population II--Stages 2 and 3

Variable	Type of School				Total U.S.	
	White		Black			
Location of Residence[a]						
Percent Urban	17	(8)	89	(65)	27	(21)
Percent Rural	18	(23)	0	(35)	15	(17)
Percent Urban and Suburban	16	(10)	0	(0)	16	(15)
Enrollment						
Average number of boys	452	(415)	817	(553)	512	(453)
Average number of girls	428	(389)	811	(567)	490	(429)
Average Size of Faculty	45.7	(45.1)	78.7	(53.2)	52.5	(45.5)
Percent Male Teachers	46.8	(39.5)	41.6	(47.2)	48.3	(41.1)
Personnel Services Provided						
Percent Having a Librarian	95		100		97	
Percent Having a Guidance Counselor	91		100		95	
Percent Having a School Psychologist	30		25		29	
Percent Having a Reading Specialist	54		89		61	
Percent Having Teacher Aides	47		17		42	

[a] See note to Table 41.

show considerably greater use of paraprofessionals. The generally higher level of services in the predominantly black schools may stem in part from their urban character as well as from special federal financial programs that are intended to furnish such services to schools that have substantial numbers of students from homes that are classified as disadvantaged (see data on Father's Occupation in Tables 45 and 46).

Tables 43 and 44 present data on a number of characteristics of teachers in white and black schools at both population levels. With very few exceptions, the teachers and teaching practices in the white and black schools are quite similar. The few items that do show differences do not seem to be especially noteworthy except for the percent of teachers, at Population I, expressing a feeling of restriction on their freedom to teach. 12% of the teachers in the white schools report feeling a sense of restriction, compared with 40% of the teachers in the black schools. This may be because the majority of schools with predominantly black enrollments are located in an urban setting, and large urban school systems tend to place more emphasis on a syllabus or course of study.

Tables 45 and 46 present data on selected characteristics of students in white and black schools at the two population levels. Again, the notable finding is the similarity between students in the two kinds of schools. The sole exception is father's occupation. At both

Table 43

Selected Characteristics of Teachers in White and
Black Schools at Population I--Stage 2

Variable	Type of School		Total U.S.
	White	Black	
Years of Teaching Experience			
Percent less than 5 years	34	28	33
Percent 5-10 years	22	21	23
Percent more than 10 years	44	51	44
Time Spent Each Week in Planning			
Percent less than 3 hours	9	7	8
Percent between 3-6 hours	43	36	46
Percent more than 6 hours	48	57	46
Time Spent Each Week in Marking Papers			
Percent less than 3 hours	14	10	18
Percent between 3-6 hours	46	53	49
Percent more than 6 hours	40	37	33
Grouping of Students Within a Classroom			
Percent always or almost always	20	44	21
Percent frequently	42	39	40
Percent occasionally	28	16	27
Percent rarely or never	10	1	12
Percent Feeling Restrictions on Freedom to Teach	12	40	14
Percent Feeling that Facilities and Equipment are Limited	75	93	73

Table 44

Selected Characteristics of Teachers in White and
Black Schools at Population II--Stages 2 and 3

Variable	Type of School		Total U.S.
	White	Black	
Years of Teaching Experience			
Percent less than 5 years	32 (37)	48 (80)	38 (37)
Percent 5-10 years	25 (25)	25 (9)	26 (25)
Percent more than 10 years	43 (38)	27 (12)	37 (38)
Time Spent Each Week in Planning			
Percent less than 3 hours	7 (6)	9 (0)	7 (7)
Percent between 3-6 hours	37 (30)	41 (9)	37 (26)
Percent between 6-10 hours	56 (64)	5 (91)	56 (67)
Time Spent Each Week in Marking Papers			
Percent less than 3 hours	14 (17)	13 (41)	14 (14)
Percent between 3-6 hours	48 (45)	55 (26)	49 (50)
Percent between 6-10 hours	38 (38)	32 (33)	26 (36)
Grouping of Students Within a Classroom			
Percent frequently	13 (10)	24 (22)	13 (10)
Percent occasionally	36 (25)	47 (9)	36 (29)
Percent rarely or never	47 (64)	28 (70)	17 (60)
Percent Feeling Restrictions on Freedom to Teach	21	21	20
Percent Feeling that Facilities and Equipment are Limited	77	82	75

population levels, the number of students in the predominantly black schools who did not answer the item on father's occupation was quite high—46% and 31% at Populations I and II, respectively, in Stage 2, and 19% at Population II in Stage 3. Of the students who did respond, the percentage of students reporting that their father's occupation was at the professional or managerial level was substantially greater in white schools than in black schools—28% versus 7% at Population I, 35% versus 13% at Population II in Stage 2, and 38% versus 12% at Population II in Stage 3. Differences in proportions of father's occupations in the category of Clerical and Sales Workers were also sizable. It is clear that the students in the predominantly black schools

Table 45

Selected Characteristics of Students in White and
Black Schools at Population I

Variable	Type of School		Total U.S.
	White	Black	
Percent Male Students	51	46	51
Average Age of Students	10.6	10.7	10.6
Father's Occupation			
Percent Professional and Managerial	28	7	25
Percent Clerical and Sales	13	6	12
Percent Skilled Workers	27	20	24
Percent Semi-skilled and Unskilled	19	21	18
Family Size			
Percent only children	3	5	4
Percent one sibling	19.	13	20
Percent Two siblings	24	18	23
Percent Three siblings	22	14	20
Number of Books in Home			
Percent fewer than 11 books	6	5	9
Percent 11-25 books	9	18	10
Percent 26-50 books	18	20	17
Average Number of Hours Spent Reading for Pleasure Each Week	2.2	2.0	1.8
Average Number of Hours of Homework Each Week	4.4	4.8	4.5

came from a lower socioeconomic level than did the students in the predominantly white schools. This is true for both population levels. Interestingly enough, however, this is the only major difference between the groups.

Tables 47 and 48 present data on student performance on the various achievement tests used in the IEA studies. Students in predominantly white schools performed significantly and substantially higher than did students in predominantly black schools on *all* tests at both Populations I and II in both stages. The difference in performance

Table 46

Selected Characteristics of Students in White and
Black Schools at Population II--Stages 2 and 3

Variable	Type of School				Total U.S.	
	White		Black			
Percent Male Students	48	(51)	43	(36)	47	(52)
Average Age of Students	14.7	(14.9)	14.7	(14.8)	14.6	(14.9)
Father's Occupation						
Percent Professional or Managerial	35	(38)	13	(12)	32	(36)
Percent Clerical and Sales	11	(8)	7	(5)	10	(10)
Percent Skilled Workers	30	(26)	27	(24)	28	(25)
Percent Semi-skilled and Unskilled	18	(22)	22	(40)	17	(21)
Family Size						
Percent only children	4		7		4	(5)
Percent one sibling	17		14		17	(19)
Percent two siblings	24		17		23	(24)
Percent three siblings	21		18		21	(20)
Number of Books in Home						
Percent fewer than 11 books	4	(2)	13	(5)	4	(5)
Percent 11-25 books	7	(6)	12	(6)	8	(7)
Percent 26-50 books	18	(14)	21	(17)	18	(16)
Average Number of Hours Spent Reading for Pleasure Each Week	2.0	(2.0)	1.7	(1.9)	1.8	(2.0)
Average Number of Hours of Homework Each Week	5.7	(6.3)	5.3	(5.4)	5.7	(5.9)

between students in the two types of schools ranges from one-third of a
standard deviation (Civic Education at Population II) to more than one
standard deviation (Science achievement at both populations). Furthermore, the difference in performance between the groups in Stage 2 on
the Word Knowledge Test, a verbal ability test, is about the same as
the difference between the groups on the achievement tests.

The smallest difference between the groups is in Reading Speed.
Since the same Reading Speed Test was used at both population levels,
it is possible to note the difference between the levels for each group.
For both black and white schools, students at Population II perform
about 0.9 of a standard deviation above students at the Population II
level. That is, the amount of increase in performance from one age
level to another is almost the same for both groups (the difference of

Table 47

Means and Standard Deviations for Selected Tests
at Population I

Variable	Type of School		Total U.S.
	White	Black	
Science			
Mean	19.8	8.3	17.7
S.D.	8.4	7.6	9.2
Reading Comprehension			
Mean	18.6	7.8	16.8
S.D.	11.3	9.1	11.5
Reading Speed			
Mean	25.4	21.4	24.7
S.D.	8.1	9.9	8.6
Word Knowledge			
Mean	19.1	8.5	17.4
S.D.	10.4	9.8	11.2

0.06 standard deviations between the increases for the two groups is inconsequential).

SUMMARY

It is difficult to draw any firm conclusions about the differences in performance between schools with predominantly white and predominantly black student populations. Race was not a stratifying variable in the sampling plan for the United States, so attempts to generalize results beyond the sample of schools actually studied is not possible. Second, the considerable confounding of race and social status as indicated by reported occupation of the father makes it impossible to say anything about performance differences other than the fact that they do exist. Perhaps the most noteworthy finding is the negligible differences between schools in so many of the variables describing the schools and the teachers. It would appear that, compared with ten and

Table 48

Means and Standard Deviations for Selected Tests
at Population II--Stages 2 and 3

| Variable | Type of School | | Total U.S. |
	White	Black	
Science			
Mean	22.6	12.5	21.5
S.D.	11.3	9.1	11.6
Reading Comprehension			
Mean	29.4	16.5	27.3
S.D.	10.5	11.6	11.6
Reading Speed			
Mean	33.0	29.5	32.4
S.D.	6.8	9.4	7.3
Word Knowledge			
Mean	17.9 (16.3)	10.2 (11.5)	16.8 (16.3)
S.D.	8.4 (9.4)	8.5 (8.2)	8.8 (9.6)
Literature			
Mean	17.5	10.9	16.5
S.D.	8.4	8.8	8.8
Civic Education			
Mean	23.6	21.4	24.7
S.D.	9.6	9.2	9.9

twenty years ago, considerable progress has been made in equalizing educational opportunity between the various racial groups in the United States. Test performance differences do, however, persist.

Chapter 6

The Regression Analyses

Because the various IEA studies were conceived and carried out as
separate enterprises, one for each subject matter area, it was decided
that the bulk of the analyses should be conducted separately by subject.
Some cross-subject analyses were in fact carried out, notably in
Science, Literature, and Reading Comprehension, but these were
modest by comparison with the within-subject analyses. Furthermore,
since testing within each subject area was conducted separately at the
three population levels, analyses were carried out for each level
separately.

The studies were multi-national as opposed to cross-national.
That is, countries were viewed as replications. Thus, if a particular
variable was found to be related to achievement in a particular subject
area in, say, twelve out of fifteen countries, this was taken as evidence
of a universally important variable within the domain of countries
under study. On the other hand, a variable that was found to be related
to achievement in only one or two countries was given less attention.
This does not mean that the variable might not be of importance within
a particular country—it might well be. The research team was,
however, searching for variables that the analyses showed to be
important in a number of countries.

The IEA investigations were guided by a number of hypotheses,
both explicit and implicit. Variables that were likely to be related to
achievement in each subject area were identified and measures were
developed for each. In a number of cases there were single questionnaire items or groups of items; in other cases scales were developed,
and in still other cases tests were constructed. These were then
organized into various questionnaires, tests, and scales. Students were
administered all three kinds of instruments; teachers and school
officials, usually principals, completed questionnaires and, in a few
cases, responded to some scales. In general, there was a genuine
attempt to obtain a measure for every variable hypothesized to be

related to achievement in a subject matter area. In some cases, this was fairly easy, e.g., determining the sex of the student. In other cases, however, it was much harder. Obtaining a measure of the climate or ambience of a school is exceedingly difficult. The practical limitations of survey research are generally well known. In many cases, the measures were partial and indirect indicators rather than direct measures of the variables of interest. The crudeness of measurement of some variables was also a problem. To include an item on a questionnaire in a mass survey often requires that a set of categories be provided so that the individual can select the appropriate category of response. If the variable covers a broad range, which most of the variables did because the variability over countries was considerable, then the crudity of the categories may mask important differences.

The primary statistical procedure for analyzing the data was multiple regression analysis. Two major kinds of regression analyses were carried out—between pupils and between schools. In the former, the student served as the unit of analysis; school and teacher data, aggregated for the school, were added to each student's record to obtain a correlation matrix. In the between-schools analyses, all data for a school were aggregated into series of means or percentages to create a school record, which was used to produce a correlation matrix. Before this could be done, however, three problems had to be dealt with. First, variables that were categorical had to be transformed into a linear scale. Second, unique national measures of international variables had to be handled appropriately. Third, a considerable reduction in the number of variables had to be made before the correlation matrix was produced and the regressions performed.

The procedure used for scaling such categorical variables as father's occupation was criterion scaling (Mayeske, et al., 1970). For each country's k categories of father's occupation, $k - 1$ dummy variables were created and a regression analysis was carried out at Population II. This resulted in a set of weights that maximized the predictive effectiveness of father's occupation with the Reading Comprehension Test score. The scale values for each country's Population II students were then applied to its Population I and IV students for all criterion measures of achievement. It was believed that this would provide the most appropriate scaling because, on the one hand, Population II students were considered to be mature enough to supply accurate information about their father's occupation and, on the other hand, the sample of Population II students covered the whole range of occupational levels and student ability because schooling was still officially compulsory in all the participating countries at this age. The second problem, the inclusion of unique national measures of international variables, required no special treatment since all regression analyses were carried out within a country at each population level. Thus, the fact that each country used a set of unique categories for father's occupation had no bearing on the results.

The third problem, selecting the variables to be included in the correlation matrix and the regression analysis, was a critical one. Data were available for over 750 variables. Computing a correlation matrix of that size for each population level for each subject area in each country would have been exceedingly expensive. Furthermore, since testing had been carried out in from 125 to 272 schools at each population level for each subject area in the United States, and in about one hundred schools in each other country, there was a problem of degrees of freedom in carrying out the between-schools analyses. The problem was resolved in two ways: compositing and screening. Compositing of variables was done partly on rational bases and partly on an *a priori* basis. On an *a priori* basis, variables were first divided into four categories:

1. Block 1—Background variables, primarily indicators of home and family conditions but including sex and age. These represented prior conditions of the student, his family, and his community.
2. Block 2—Type of school or type of program in which the student was enrolled. This was a general indicator of previous learning conditions.
3. Block 3—School variables: Including curricular and instructional organization and procedures, and teacher characteristics and behavior.
4. Block 4—Kindred variables representing present characteristics of students—their activities, interests, and attitudes. These were viewed as concomitants of achievement rather than as causes.

Within each category, certain variables appeared to go together logically. For example, in Reading Comprehension, several questionnaire items that dealt with the availability of reading resources were grouped together. Similarly, father's and mother's education, and father's occupation were combined into an index of socioeconomic status of the home. Weights for combining variables into composites were generally determined by pooling correlational data from a number of countries and then determining weights that would, on average, best predict the achievement criterion under study.

In some cases, further compositing was done. A School Handicap Score was created for each country by weighting the following variables in combination for all populations:

1. Father's occupation
2. Number of books in home
3. Use of dictionary in the home
4. Number of siblings (reversed scaling)

and at Populations II and IV:

5. Father's education
6. Mother's education.

Thus, some reduction in the number of variables was achieved by combining them into clusters on either a logical or an empirical basis.

At the same time, a screening exercise was undertaken. Both single variables and composites were studied in relation to each criterion measure. These relationships were examined either as calculated (zero order correlations) or with one or more background factors, e.g., socioeconomic status of the family, and type of school or program partialled out. In this analysis, countries were regarded as replications and attention was focused primarily on relationships that were consistent in all or almost all of the countries in the study. When the relationship between a particular variable and a criterion varied from one country to another with correlations about evenly balanced between positive and negative and also quite small, it was generally regarded as zero and the variable was usually eliminated from the analysis. It is, of course, possible that the measure had a variable and balanced opposite significance from country to country. A more plausible explanation, however, is that the variations represented only chance fluctuations around a near zero "true" value. It seemed better to eliminate the variable rather than try to explain such variations. A number of variables were eliminated through this screening procedure, especially when input factors representing home conditions and socioeconomic status had been partialled out. Variables that were eliminated in this manner included class size, availability of specialist teachers, guidance counselors, etc. Those variables that showed some promise empirically or were of special interest on logical grounds were retained.

A second screening was then made using the school handicap score as a control variable. For the between-schools analyses, the variables entering into a composite were averages based on all pupils tested in a school. Variables that added nothing to the prediction of the criterion beyond what was available on the basis of the input variables alone were eliminated from further analysis. Approximately 30 to 40 variables were retained for the final regression analyses in each subject at each population level.

The international volumes present summary results of the regression analyses. Stress is placed on those variables and blocks of variables that behave similarly from country to country. In this volume, attention is focused on the full results for the United States. Before these results are presented, however, two points need to be made. The first involves the order of entry of the blocks of variables into the regression model and the second the interpretations that can and cannot be made of the results.

The order of entry of variables is a temporal one. Home variables are entered first in the regression equation since they represent the earliest influences on the student. Type of program is entered second since it is to some extent a reflection of success achieved in earlier learning. The block of school variables is entered third since these represent the present conditions of the school and the instructional variables. The kindred variables are entered last since it is often not clear whether they are causes of the achievement to be explained, effects of that achievement, or correlates of the achievement, the nature of whose relationship with achievement is largely not known.

The issue of order of entry of variables (or, more correctly, blocks of variables) is critical because the predictor variables in the correlation matrix are typically substantially correlated. Thus, the order of entry of variables makes a considerable difference in the proportion of the variance of the criterion variable that is assigned to each block. Consider, for example, the following illustration of a correlation matrix showing the relationships between height of fathers, height of mothers, and height of children.

	Variables	
	2	3
1. Height of father	.6	.5
2. Height of mother		.5
3. Height of child		1.0

25% of the variance in children's height is statistically explained by the height of the father ($r^2 = .25$). Similarly, 25% of the children's height is explained by the height of the mother. The multiple correlation of children's height with father's and mother's height is .55; the variance in children's height accounted for by both parents is .31. If the father's height is entered into the regression equation first, it accounts for 25%, and the mother's contribution is 6%. If the order of entry is reversed, the contributions are reversed. With non-zero correlations between predictor variables, the variables that enter into the regression equation first take the largest bite out of the explainable variance; those that enter later are left with less to explain. This is precisely what has happened in the regression analyses of the IEA studies and indeed what happens in all regression analyses in which the regression equation is built up by the accretion of variables or groups of variables. The rationale for the order of entry is essentially a temporal one and is discussed in detail in the technical volume (Peaker, 1975). It is noted here because of its effect on the proportions of variance that are assigned to the various blocks.

The second major point concerns the interpretation of the results of the regression analyses. Multiple regression analysis attempts to explain statistically variation in a criterion variable (in this study, achievement test performance) by relating it to the variations in a set of predictor variables. The explanation that is sought is statistical, not causal. Furthermore, the magnitude of the relationship of a predictor variable or a set of predictor variables with a criterion variable can be considerably affected by the amount of variability in the predictor(s). In the most extreme case, a predictor variable that has no variability whatsoever will show a zero relationship with the criterion. It may, however, be extremely important causally. For example, teachers who have had a uniform amount of training may contribute mightily to the education of their students, but amount of training will in fact show no relationship to student performance. Multiple regression analysis is intended to "explain" statistically *variations* in student performance; it does not explain the *level* of performance. Regression analyses of school achievement are influenced by this phenomenon, because although we allow homes to range from very good to very bad, very bad schools are not allowed to exist. Certification and accreditation standards, coupled with community, state, and even federal controls, are intended to ensure that certain minimal standards of education are met. This reduces the amount of variability of school-related variables. The reader is thus cautioned against interpreting the absence of relationships as the absence of effects signifying that schooling is of little importance.

Chapter 7

Between-School Differences
in Achievement

This chapter presents the results of the between-schools regression analyses for Science, Reading Comprehension, and Literature for the United States. Limitations of time and money prevented carrying out similar analyses for French and Civic Education.

Three points need to be made about the between-schools analyses. First, the school is the basic unit of analysis. This presents no problem whatsoever for variables obtained from the school questionnaire, where a single response such as extent of coeducation holds for the whole school. For teacher and student data, the case is rather different. Data from all teachers and students who responded to the instruments have been aggregated to characterize the school. In some cases, this has taken the form of school averages, such as the average score on an achievement test. In other cases, percentages have been obtained, such as the percent of science teachers in the school who are male. Because students within a school tend to be more similar to one another than to students in different schools, relationships between a predictor and a criterion variable are increased through the use of a unit of anlysis that combines individual cases. This effect, commonly referred to as the ecological or contextual effect, poses no real problems in the analysis of the data (see Blalock, 1964). It does, however, affect the interpretations one makes of the results. For this reason, the reader is asked to consider the results of the regression analyses presented in this chapter along with those presented in the next chapter, where the individual student is the unit of analysis. Taken together, the results of the two sets of analyses present a balanced picture of the results of the study.

A second point that needs to be emphasized is that a predictor variable enters into the regression analysis only when there is sufficient variation in the variable and such variation is related to variation in the criterion variable of achievement. If there is insufficient variability in a variable, it has no chance to enter into the analysis. Age of entry to school is an example of such a variable. In the United States, age of entry is almost uniformly six years of age (the policy is quite clear, the execution varies). Thus, this variable cannot enter into a regression analysis because there is insufficient variation to allow it to correlate with any achievement measure. This is not to say that it may not be an important determiner of a student's level of achievement. It may or may not; it simply cannot be detected in a regression analysis.

The third point to emphasize is that the intercorrelations among the predictor variables make it virtually impossible to estimate the contribution of each predictor variable to explaining the variance of a criterion variable. The temporal order of entry assigns the lion's share of the explainable variance in the criterion variable to those predictors that enter early in the analysis. This means that the effects of later entrants in the analysis are probably underestimated. Thus, the effects of learning condition variables should be viewed as minimum estimates.

PRESENTATION OF THE REGRESSION ANALYSES

The form of presentation of the regression analyses requires some explanation since the organization and some features of it may be unfamiliar. The large number of variables have been grouped into four blocks. The first block comprises variables related to the community setting in which the school is located, the general socioeconomic level of the homes from which the students come, and some of the personal characteristics of the students in the sample. Examples of variables that are included in the regression equation from this block include the School Handicap Score, sex of students or, more appropriately, the sex composition of the sample of students tested, and average age of the students tested.

The second block comprises two variables, type of school and type of program in which students are enrolled. In many countries where there is a variety of specialized schools and a considerable amount of selection and placement of students, type of school is an important predictor of school achievement. In the United States, however, where multi-purpose comprehensive schools predominate, type of school is an irrelevant variable. Accordingly, for the United States, community type, as determined from the sampling plan, was criterion scaled against reading comprehension and a set of weights were determined so that a composite could be formed from the various categories of community type. Thus, the type of school variable can be considered more as an indicator of the setting in which the school is located than as a measure of the school itself.

Type of program is based on information reported by students in Populations II and IV on the course of studies they were following. In the United States, the three main categories of program were academic, vocational or commercial, and general. These too were criterion scaled against reading comprehension, and the resulting weights were used to aggregate the information for all students in the sample tested in each school. Type of program was considered to be a key variable at the Population II and IV levels (the question was not asked at Population I because of the lack of differentiation) because it represented the student's present placement in the educational structure, which is a direct result of his prior educational experiences.

The third block comprises those variables representing the present conditions of learning, although there are one or two exceptions. Curricular and instructional variables, organizational features of the school, and characteristics of the teachers comprise the bulk of the variables in this block. The average grade level of the students in the sample, however, was included in this block. Technically, the grade level of students is more properly regarded as an indicator of the students' previous learning experiences than of their present ones. Its inclusion in the block of present learning condition variables was inadvertent.

The last block contains the kindred variables. These are concomitants of achievement whose relationship to the criterion are largely unknown. It was thus decided to enter them last, after the variables describing the present conditions of learning had been entered.

The results of the various regression analyses are presented in Tables 49 through 56. The form of presentation in all tables is the same. Variables entering into the regression equation are presented by blocks. Variables that entered into the regression equation at an early stage, e.g., in the first block, but were removed at a later stage because of the addition of other variables, have been omitted. If no variables from a particular block were included in the model, that block has been omitted. Thus, in Table 49, Type of Community/Program is omitted since neither of the variables in that block met the criterion for inclusion (that criterion was $F = 2.0$, a somewhat lenient value; see Peaker, 1975, p. 61).

Several items of information are provided for each variable included in the equation. The first item is the simple correlation (r) between the variable and the criterion. The second item is the weight

(*Wt.*) for the variable in the full regression equation. This is the standardized regression coefficient, or beta weight, and indicates the weight accorded the variable in the full regression equation. The third item is the Unique Contribution to R^2. This is the amount by which R^2 would be increased if the variable were entered as the final one in the regression model. Additionally, the multiple correlation (R) and the percentage of variance of the criterion variable that has been accounted for by all variables entered so far (R^2) are given for each block. Simple subtraction allows one to estimate the increase in R or R^2 for any block of variables. The values of R and R^2 at the end of the last block denote the final multiple correlation and the total percentage of variance in the criterion variable that is accounted for by all the predictors. The last item of information is the sum of the unique contributions to the final R^2. Subtracting this total from the final R^2 yields the amount of joint variation among the predictor variables. In many cases, the total of the unique contributions to R^2 is a small fraction of the final R^2.[1]

---

[1]Detailed explanations about each item of information that is presented can be found in any statistical text dealing with multiple regression analysis. One of the best available sources is F. Kerlinger and E. Pedhazur, *Multiple regression in behavioral research* (New York: Holt, Rinehart and Winston, 1973). For the lay reader, the following abbreviated explanations are offered.

Simple correlation is the Pearson-product moment correlation coefficient. This is an index number describing the extent of statistical association between two variables. In the present study, the simple correlations describe the association between a particular predictor variable and an achievement criterion. The range of values a simple correlation can take varies from -1.00 to $+1.00$. The higher the value of the simple correlation, regardless of sign, the greater the relationship between the two variables. A positive correlation indicates that an increase in the value of one variable is associated with an increase in the value of the other variable; a negative correlation indicates that an increase in the value of one variable is associated with a decrease in the value of another variable.

Weight refers to the regression weight accorded a variable in determining the best straight-line equation for predicting performance on the achievement variable under study. The higher the value of the weight for a variable, regardless of sign, the greater its contribution in determining the predicted achievement level. Ordinarily, the numerical value of the weight is less than the value of the simple correlation because the value of the weight is based on an analysis involving all variables, whereas the simple correlation involves only a single predictor variable and the achievement criterion.

In most cases, the sign of the simple correlation and the weight will be the same. Reversals can and do occur, however. That is, the sign of the simple correlation and the regression weight for a variable can differ. In Table 51, for example, student reports about the amount of interest their parents express in their progress in school is positively related to their science achievement $(r = +.17)$. This variable has a weight of $-.24$, however, indicating that when all other variables are considered, parental interest must be weighted negatively to best predict science achievement. The reader is alerted to the fact that there are a number of sign reversals in both the between-schools and between-students analyses. In such cases, the sign of the simple correlation denotes the direction of the relationship between the predictor variable and the achievement criterion under study, whereas the sign of the regression coefficient denotes the direciton of the contribution to maximum prediction of the criterion when all other variables are considered.

Table 49

Results of Between-Schools Regression Analysis for Science--
Population I

Blocks and Variables	r	Wt.	Unique Contri-bution to R²	R	R²
I Background					
School Handicap Score	.81	.53	.122		
Sex of students	-.10	-.09	.008	.82	.67
III Learning Conditions					
Design own experiments	-.35	-.17	.025		
Grade	.05	.10	.008		
Regular science lessons	.39	.07	.003		
Frequency of PTA meetings	-.04	-.12	.012		
Frequency of use of audio- visual materials	.03	.12	.013		
Observations and experiments	.48	.06	.002	.86	.75
IV Kindreds					
School motivation scale	.59	.27	.034		
Like science scale	-.12	-.15	.015		
Hours of TV per day	-.36	-.06	.003		
Hours reading for pleasure per week	.29	.05	.003		
		Total	.249	.89	.79

SCIENCE

Population I

The results of the between-schools regression analysis for Science for Population I are presented in Table 49. The largest part of the predicted variance in Science achievement is accounted for by the variables in Block I. The School Handicap Score's simple correlation with Science achievement is +.81, quite close to the final multiple correlation of +.89. The entry of the School Handicap Score accounts for so much of the explainable variance that there is little left to account for. The sex composition of the school samples has a small independent effect. Since males were coded as 1 and females as 2 in order to compute correlations, the negative simple correlation with Science achievement may be interpreted as saying that schools with higher percentages of boys perform better than schools with lower percentages of boys.

There is no contribution to the model by variables in Block II. Six variables in Block III make some contribution toward explaining the variation in Science achievement. Four of them are clearly instructional variables. "Design own experiments" was a questionnaire item in which students were asked to report whether their teachers provided an opportunity for them to make up their own problems and design their own experiments. Students replied "yes" or "no," which were coded as 1 and 2, respectively. Thus, the negative simple correlation indicates that more opportunity for student-initiated activities is associated with lower levels of achievement. Also, higher achievement is associated with having regular science lessons, performing experiments and making observations of scientific phenomena, and the use of audio-visual materials in science, although the simple correlation of this last variable with Science achievement is negligible. Grade in school, which is more an indicator of previous learning, and the infrequency of PTA meetings have small simple correlations with Science achievement and round out the list of Block III variables.

The Block IV variables showed some sizable simple correlations with achievement but collectively accounted for only an additional 3% of the variation in Science achievement scores. Two of the variables were affective measures. The School Motivation Scale comprised eleven items, which were defined to range from "a lack of effort and involvement in school and school learning" to "a high level of industry and participation in school work and a desire to succeed in school learning." This scale was eventually used only at the Population I level. Its simple correlation with Science achievement was

Table 50

Results of Between-Schools Regression Analysis for Science--
Population II

Blocks and Variables	r	Wt.	Unique Contri- bution to R²	R	R²
I Background					
School Handicap Score	.78	.58	.169		
Age	.08	.08	.005		
Sex of students	-.26	-.11	.010	.82	.67
III Learning Conditions					
Percent male teachers	.22	.23	.037		
Opportunity to learn science	.16	.16	.022		
Homework in science	.53	.13	.008		
School environment scale	.49	.12	.010		
Science study	.27	.03	.001	.88	.78
IV Kindreds					
Science attitudes	.37	.12	.011		
Hours per week reading for pleasure	.51	.09	.005		
Total			.278	.89	.79

second only to the School Handicap Score. The Like School Scale comprised twelve items designed to assess the students' personal liking for school. Its small negative simple correlation with Science achievement is somewhat puzzling but consistent with results obtained from the use of virtually the same set of items in the previous study of mathematics achievement (Husén, 1967, p. 38). Hours of TV watched per day and hours of reading for pleasure per week had moderate negative and positive simple correlations with achievement, respectively. What these results indicate is that students who watch a considerable amount of TV per day tend to score lower on the Science test than do students who watch little or no TV each day; students who spend a fair amount of time reading for pleasure each week tend to perform better on the Science tests than do students who spend little or no time in reading for pleasure. The unique contributions of the variables in Block IV is, however, rather small.

Population II

The regression analysis results for science for Population II are presented in Table 50. The background variables in Block I again account for the major share of the variance in Science achievement test scores and, of the variables in the block, the School Handicap Score is again the most potent predictor ($r = .78$). The average age of students and sex of students make small independent contributions. In the case of age, the simple correlation indicates that, within the age range 14.0 to 14.11, older students tend to perform slightly better than younger students ($r = .08$). This is undoubtedly due to the fact that the older students are in the ninth grade and the younger students are in the eighth grade. Sex of students, as in Population I, shows a characteristic negative correlation with Science achievement, indicating that the boys perform better than the girls.

No Block II variables entered into the regression model. In Block III, higher achievement is associated with having a high proportion of male teachers in the school, having the opportunity to learn the material that is included in the Science test, receiving more homework in science, and currently taking science as well as having studied a considerable amount of science previously. The last variable, School Environment, was a scale that comprised a set of items describing the degree of flexibility (high scores) as contrasted with the degree of rigidity (low scores) with which students view the learning of subject matter within the school. Collectively, the five Block III variables

Table 51

Results of Between-Schools Regression Analysis for Science--
Population IV

Blocks and Variables	r	Wt.	Unique Contri- bution to R^2	R	R^2
I Background					
School Handicap Score	.60	.66	.30		
Sex of students	-.17	-.18	.03		
				.66	.44
III Learning Conditions					
Science study	.54	.30	.05		
Teachers' training	-.12	.13	.01		
School enrollment	.17	.09	.01		
Total science homework	.46	.11	.01		
				.79	.63
IV Kindreds					
Parents' interest	.17	-.24	.04		
Science attitudes	.41	.21	.03		
			Total .48	.83	.69

account for 11% of the variance in Science test scores after the background variables have been entered.

In Block IV, two variables entered the regression. Science attitudes was a composite variable consisting of the students' reported interest and activities in science, their views on the importance of science in the world, and a view that mathematics was important in learning science. Hours of reading for pleasure per week also entered into this block. Although the simple correlation of this last variable was substantial ($r = .51$), its unique contribution to R^2 was negligible because of its relationship with other variables. Taken together, the two variables in Block IV add only 1% to the explanation of the variance of the Science test scores.

Population IV

Table 51 presents the results of the regression analysis for Science for Population IV. Again, the Block I variables, notably the School Handicap Score, account for the largest share of the variance in the Science test scores. Sex of students enters in the same way as in Population I and II. No Block II variables entered into the model.

Four variables from Block III collectively account for 19% of the variance in the Science test scores after the Block I variables have been entered. Science study, a composite of currently taking science and amount of science currently and previously studied, has a sizable simple correlation ($r = .54$) with Science achievement but, strictly speaking, cannot be considered a measure of present learning conditions. It does, however, indicate a definite school effect, independent of home background, on Science achievement. The variable with the second highest simple correlation with Science achievement is total number of hours of science homework per week ($r = .46$). The interpretation of this relationship is straightforward. School enrollment has a modest correlation with achievement, perhaps indicating that larger schools offer a greater number and variety of science learning experiences than do smaller schools. The amount of training of the science teachers has an unexpectedly negative, albeit low, correlation with Science achievement. Before engaging in any interpretation of this aberrant finding, one should perhaps note that since certification requirements specify certain minimum amounts of training in science, the variation in this variable is rather restricted. Thus, one might merely note the low negative relationship between the amount of variation in teacher training in science beyond required minima and the Science achievement of students, but attempt no interpretation.

Table 52

Results of Between-Schools Regression Analysis for Reading
Comprehension--Population I

Blocks and Variables	r	Wt.	Unique Contri- bution to R²	R	R²
I Background					
School Handicap Score	.79	.58	.165	.79	.63
II Type of Community/program					
Type of community	.37	.08	.006	.80	.64
III Learning Conditions					
Teach reading as part of instruction in English	-.29	-.14	.019		
Grade	.13	.13	.015	.84	.70
IV Kindreds					
School motivation	.62	.23	.024		
Like school	-.07	-.11	.009		
Hours of TV per day	-.37	-.09	.007	.86	.73
Total			.245		

Two variables in Block IV account for 6% of the variation in Science test scores. Parental interest in the students' learning and progress in school and the science attitudes and interests of the student are both positively related to achievement and make small independent contributions to R^2.

Unlike Populations I and II, where the unique contribution to R^2 of the variables accounted for less than one-third of the explained variance, almost 70% of the explained variation in Science test scores at Population IV is due to the unique contributions of the variables. This may be due to the fact that at Population IV the range of home backgrounds is somewhat reduced because of school dropouts. Evidence for this possible explanation appears in the simple correlation of the School Handicap Score with Science achievement— +.60 at Population IV, and +.81 and +.78 at Populations I and II, respectively.

READING COMPREHENSION

Population I

The results of the regression analysis for Reading Comprehension for Population I are presented in Table 52. The School Handicap Score is the only Block I variable that enters into the regression equation. Its contribution, however, is enormous; it has a simple correlation of +.79 with Reading Comprehension, contrasted with the final multiple correlation of .86. Type of community, a Block II variable, makes a small independent contribution, increasing the multiple correlation to .80. This, of course, leaves little variation in reading comprehension scores to be explained by the variables in the remaining blocks.

Two variables from Block III enter the regression model. The first variable, "Teach reading as part of instruction in English," was based on reports of teachers as to whether they taught reading as part of general English instruction. An affirmative answer was coded as 1 and a negative answer as 2. Thus, the negative simple correlation ($r = -.29$) between this variable and Reading Comprehension scores indicates that teachers who did not incorporate reading instruction into general English instruction but rather taught reading separately had higher scoring pupils than did teachers who reported incorporating reading instruction into general English instruction. It would appear from this result that if one wants to improve reading comprehension, direct instruction separated from other aspects of language arts is desirable. The other variable in Block III that entered into the regression model is grade in school. This variable, however, is more an indicator of previous than of present learning conditions.

Three variables in Block IV entered into the regression model. The previously described School Motivation Scale has a substantial simple correlation with Reading Comprehension ($r = +.62$); it is clearly a concomitant of Reading Comprehension. The Like School Scale has a rather small negative relationship with Reading Comprehension ($r = -.07$). The relationship of this variable with achievement is again puzzling and no easy interpretation is possible. Hours of TV watched per day has a moderate negative correlation ($r = -.37$) with achievement, suggesting that students who watch a good deal of TV per day score lower than do students who watch relatively little TV per day.

The final multiple correlation of .86 is about as high as one could expect given errors of measurement in both the predictor and criterion variables. The home background of students, as represented by the School Handicap Score, explains so much of the variation in the test scores that, once entered, there is little left to be explained. The unique contribution of the variables, however, is about one-third of the total explained variance in the Reading Comprehension test scores.

Population II

The results of the regression analysis for Population II are presented in Table 53 and are rather similar to those found in Population I. The background variables in Block I again account for the bulk of the variation in Reading Comprehension test performance; the main contributor is the School Handicap Score, which has a simple correlation with test performance of $+.82$. The small unique contribution of this variable to the final R^2 should be noted, however. This indicates that, not only are better readers associated with better homes, they are also associated with better learning conditions and various concomitants of reading achievement.

Four variables enter the regression equation in Block III. Grade in school, as previously noted, is a placement variable. Hours of homework per week and the School Environment Scale have substantial simple correlations with Reading Comprehension test performance ($+.60$ and $+.55$, respectively). This suggests that more homework and a climate of flexibility as opposed to rigidity in the school are important ingredients in a school program. Finally, the sex composition of the faculty has a low negative simple correlation ($r = -.08$) with test

Table 53

Results of Between-Schools Regression Analysis for Reading
Comprehension--Population II

Blocks and Variables	r	wt.	Unique contribution to R²	R	R²
I Background					
School Handicap Score	.82	.39	.048		
Age	.01	-.10	.004	.83	.69
III Learning Conditions					
Grade	.30	.20	.015		
Hours homework per week	.60	.21	.023		
School environment scale	.55	.09	.005		
Sex of teachers	-.08	-.02	.001	.86	.74
IV Kindreds					
Parent's interest	.05	-.29	.062		
Reading resources	.65	.27	.040		
Hours per week reading for pleasure	.59	.23	.031		
Total			.229	.93	.86

performance, indicating that schools with a higher percentage of male teachers have students who read slightly better than do students in schools with lower percentages of male teachers.

Three variables in Block IV entered the regression model. Parental interest in school activities and progress has a small simple correlation with Reading Comprehension test performance. Reading resources in the home, a composite variable based on ownership of a dictionary, number of books in the home, receipt of daily newspaper, and number of different magazines received in the home, had a substantial positive correlation with test performance ($r = +.65$), as did the number of hours per week spent in reading for pleasure ($r = .59$). The placement of reading resources in the block of kindred variables is somewhat arbitrary. It may be considered a background variable and, in fact, is one of the ingredients of the School Handicap Score. Its emergence in Block IV with a sizable weight attests to its singular importance for the prediction of Reading achievement.

The overall multiple correlation of .93 is about the upper limit for such a statistic considering the unreliability of both predictor and criterion variables. The relatively low proportions of unique variation accounted for by the variables (.229) indicates that background, learning conditions, and kindred variables share a considerable amount of common variance.

Population IV

Population IV results for Reading Comprehension are presented in Table 54. Unlike Populations I and II, where schooling is compulsory and there is a full range of student variability, schooling at this level is voluntary. Although the United States retains a greater proportion of an age group in school at this level than does any other country, the variability is nonetheless decreased. At Populations I and II, the variables entering into the regression analyses account for 73% and 86% of the variance in Reading Comprehension test scores, respectively, whereas only 53% of the variance is accounted for at this level.

Only two variables enter into the regression analysis at this level. The School Handicap Score, with a simple correlation of .72, enters first. The addition of the kindred, number of different magazines received in the home, increases the correlation to .73. The absence of any learning condition variables in the regression may be interpreted in several ways. On the one hand, it may be that formal instruction in reading comprehension no longer occurs at this grade level and hence

Table 54

Results of Between-Schools Regression Analysis for Reading
Comprehension--Population IV

Blocks and Variables	r	Wt.	Unique Contri-bution to R^2	R	R^2
I Background					
School Handicap Score	.72	.63	.23	.72	.52
IV Kindreds					
Magazines in the home	.55	.15	.01	.73	.53
			Total .24		

learning condition variables are simply irrelevant. On the other hand, it is possible that what instructional procedures are employed to improve reading comprehension are fairly standard and that the failure of any learning condition variables to enter into the regression analysis stems from a lack of variation in the variables studied. Other possible explanations include the failure to measure relevant instructional variables and the possibility that reading comprehension at this level is a function of verbal reasoning ability and consequently is not easily altered by instruction.

LITERATURE

Population II

The Population II results for Literature are presented in Table 55. The three background variables collectively account for 61% of the variance in the Literature test scores. Again, the School Handicap Score is the single best predictor, with a simple correlation of +.76.

Four variables from Block III enter the regression model. These are availability of a public library, the average tenure of the teachers in the school, the average number of years of training of the English teachers, and the average amount of homework per week. The first variable may more properly be considered a community resource variable, whereas the second may be more indicative of a stability factor. The average number of years of training of the teachers would appear to indicate the importance of specialized training for the teaching of literature, although the simple correlation of this variable with Literature test performance suggests the relationship is modest. Average number of hours of homework per week is a genuine instructional variable; its substantial correlation with Literature test performance ($r = .59$) suggests a definite effect. Taken together, the Block III variables account for an additional 7% of the variance in Literature test scores.

The five variables in Block IV account for an additional 17% of the variance in Literature test performance. All of the kindreds are reading related variables; their simple correlation with Literature test performance range from .34 to .65, indicating moderate to substantial relationships. Frequency of mass media is a composite variable based on student reports about the sections of the newspaper they read and the types of TV programs watched. A high score was associated with watching TV programs dealing with drama, history, nature, and science documentaries, as opposed to sports programs. Interestingly,

Table 55

Results of Between-Schools Regression Analysis for
Literature--Population II

Blocks and Variables	r	Wt.	Unique Contri-bution to R^2	R	R^2
I Background					
School Handicap Score	.76	.17	.008		
Age	.10	.08	.006		
Sex of students	.07	.09	.007	.78	.61
III Learning Conditions					
Public library	.22	.15	.022		
Years teacher at school	.11	-.01	.000		
Years of training of teacher	.20	.003	.001		
Hours of homework per week	.59	.06	.002	.82	.68
IV Kindreds					
Frequency of mass media	.44	.43	.119		
Reading resources in the home	.65	.49	.039		
Read news and comics in paper	.34	.10	.008		
Hours per week reading for pleasure	.61	.09	.005		
Reading habits--types of material chosen	.52	.07	.002	.92	.85
Total			.269		

this composite alone uniquely accounts for almost 12% of the total variation in Literature test performance. The simple correlation of reading resources in the home with Literature test performance is second only to that of the School Handicap Score; it uniquely accounts for almost 9% of the total variance in Literature test scores. Reading of the news and comic sections of the newspaper, the number of hours per week spent reading for pleasure, and reading habits or the types of materials the students select for pleasure reading round out the list of kindred variables. This last variable is a composite generated from student self-reports of the frequency with which they choose to read certain types of books. High scores are associated with reading humor, myths and legends, current events, adventure, love, and school stories. In this composite, humor is given a weight of 4, myths and legends a weight of 2, and the remainder each received a weight of 1. The high weight given to humor and its appearance as an important correlate among the sections of the newspaper that are read was unexpected and not easily explained. Taken together, the Block IV variables are indicative of reading resources, habits, and activities that show a considerable relationship with Literature test performance and, after background factors and learning condition variables have been taken into account, explain 17% of the variation in Literature test performance. The educational importance of such patterns of reading habits and activities, independent of socio-economic factors, should not be underestimated. Of the total .269 of the unique contribution of the variables to R^2, .223 comes from the Block IV variables alone. Another way of stating this is to say that education, especially in literature, is far more than schooling.

Population IV

The results of the regression analysis for Literature at Population IV are presented in Table 56. The background variables, notably the School Handicap Score, account for 32% of the variance in the Literature test scores. An additional 22% of the variance is accounted for by the Block III variables. There are five Block III variables in the analysis. The first, textbooks loaned or purchased, comes from the school questionnaire and reflects school policy on the way in which students obtain their books. This may reflect a difference between public and non-public schools rather than an instructional condition. Its correlation with the criterion is modest ($r = .10$). Hours of homework per week is, as in Population II, related to Literature performance, although the correlation of $+.16$ is substantially lower than at the

Table 56

Results of Between-Schools Regression Analysis for
Literature--Population IV

Blocks and Variables	r	Wt.	Unique Contri- bution to R²	R	R²
I Background					
School Handicap Score	.54	.55	.14		
Sex of students	.26	.16	.02	.56	.32
III Learning Conditions					
Textbooks purchased or loaned	.10	.24	.04		
Hours of homework per week	.16	-.24	.03		
Teaching load of teachers	-.34	-.18	.03		
Improve reading speed	-.27	-.10	.01		
Teacher judgment in assessing performance	-.16	-.09	.01	.73	.54
IV Kindreds					
Expected occupation and further education	.44	.25	.03		
Types of TV programs watched	.45	.17	.02		
Read about politics and economics	-.04	-.14	.01		
Literary interest scale	.09	-.12	.01		
Total			.35	.78	.60

earlier level. This may reflect both the increased homogeneity of the student population and lowered variability in the length of homework assignments. The teaching load of teachers is based on an item in the teacher questionnaire requesting the proportion of time employed in the school. Responses ranged from carrying a full-time teaching load to less than a 25% teaching load. Thus, the negative simple correlation indicates that the higher the proportion of teachers who carry a full-time teaching load, the higher the test performance of the students. "Improve reading speed" refers to intentional efforts on the part of teachers to improve their students' rate of reading. The negative simple correlation indicates that teachers who make such efforts tend to have lower scoring pupils than do teachers who do not make such efforts. This may reflect the fact that schools in which teachers make such efforts have less able students than schools in which this kind of help is not given because students do not need it. The last variable in this block, "the frequency of use of teacher judgment of general performance of students in class," has a small negative simple correlation with achievement ($r = -.16$). The item was included in the school questionnaire and was one of a number dealing with the types of appraisal procedures employed. The teacher questionnaire also contained a number of such items. The survival of this single item out of all those dealing with appraisal is interesting. It is the only item that deals with the use of observational procedures and teacher judgment in appraising student performance.

The Block IV variables, taken together, account for an additional 6% of the variation in Literature test scores. Of these, the composite of expected occupational level and amount of additional schooling, and the composite of watching TV documentaries, dramatic programs, and listening to music, correlate the highest with Literature performance and make modest unique contributions to the total R^2. Reading about politics and economics has a small negative correlation with Literature performance. Scores on the short literary interest scale show a slight positive relationship with Literature test performance but enter the regression equation with a small negative weight.

SUMMARY

It is difficult to summarize the result of eight separate regression analyses covering three different school subjects at three population levels. Some of the predictor variables entered into the regression equation for only one subject and at one population level. Others, such as hours of homework per week, recurred in several subjects and at several population levels. Obviously, variables of the latter type are far more dependable than are the singletons. The emergence of the School Handicap Score as the most potent predictor of achievement in all subjects at all population levels is clear and convincing evidence of its importance. As previously noted, however, some of its potency inheres in the fact that the categories of father's occupation, one of the ingredients of the composite, were criterion-scaled against an achievement variable, Reading Comprehension, at Population II. The School Handicap Score was also the first variable to enter into the regression. It is important to note its unique contribution to R^2 in each analysis. In all cases, this figure is considerably lower than the r^2 for School Handicap Score and achievement. This is an indication that, although the home backgrounds of students are definitely related to achievement test performance, communities with good homes tend to have good schools that contain students with the kinds of attitudes, interests, and behavior patterns associated with higher levels of performance.

An issue that has received increasing attention in recent years has been the estimation of school effects from survey data. Studies by Coleman (1966), Mayeske *et al.* (1970), Jencks (1973), and others have not fully resolved the issue. A modest attempt to clarify the issue has been made in Table 57, which gives the multiple correlation at the end of each block along with the percent of variance contributed by the variables in that block. The contributions to the explanation of variance in achievement test scores by the school effects are given under Block III. These contributions range from zero for Reading Comprehension at Population IV to 22% for Literature at the same level. The lowest level of school effect in any subject is found in Reading Comprehension. Science and Literature show definite but modest school effects. The findings in Reading Comprehension accord rather well with those of Coleman (1966). This is readily understandable when one notes that the criterion of achievement used by Coleman was the score on a verbal ability test.

It would seem that reading comprehension, like verbal ability, is a proficiency that is heavily influenced by non-school factors—the quality of the home, community resources, and the like. The lower level of school effects may be due more to the larger variability of non-school factors rather than to the lack of efficacy of relatively standard instructional programs.

In Science and Literature, direct school effects are substantially greater than in Reading Comprehension. Here the case may be that the learning of these subjects is more a function of school instruction than

Table 57

Multiple Correlations with Percent Added Variance for Blocks of
Variables for Science, Reading Comprehension, and Literature

Subject and Population	Blocks							
	I		II		III		IV	
	R	% Added Variance	R	% Added Variance	R	% Added Variance	R	% Added Variance
Science								
I	.82	67	.82	00	.86	8	.89	4
II	.82	67	.82	00	.88	11	.89	1
IV	.66	44	.66	00	.79	19	.83	6
Reading Comprehension								
I	.79	63	.80	1	.84	6	.86	3
II	.83	69	.83	00	.86	5	.93	12
IV	.72	53	.72	00	.72	00	.73	1
Literature								
II	.78	61	.78	00	.82	7	.92	17
IV	.56	32	.56	00	.73	22	.78	6

of the general cultural level of the home and the community. At Population IV, an average of 20% of the variation in test performance in both subjects is directly attributable to school factors alone.[2] Considering the order of entry of variables, which assigns all indirect effects of schooling to background factors, the real and substantial contribution of school factors should not be minimized. Public policy has been made on the basis of evidence of much weaker effects (e. g., the percentage of variation in deaths among smokers and non-smokers). At Populations I and II, the percent added variance due to school effects is somewhat lower but no less definite. It may be that at these lower levels instruction in these subjects is still in its beginning stages and its effects are not that pronounced.

Although school effects were revealed by the analyses, especially in Science and Literature, one can take little comfort in the specific variables that produced such effects. Outside of the homework variable, there was little consistency in the results. A variable that showed an independent relationship with achievement in one subject at one population level often failed to appear in the analysis at another population level in the same subject, let alone in a different subject. Educators who are seriously concerned about the identification of potent instructional variables will find the results rather unsatisfying. No single variable can be recommended to the reader for his consideration in any subject at any population level. In Reading Comprehension, there is a conspicuous absence of any malleable instructional variables. In Science and Literature, the case is somewhat different. Although no individual variable, with the exception of homework, can be pointed to, there are some categories into which the variables fall that may suggest classes of instructional variables. The general area of exposure, for example, seems to be important for Science achievement. Variables in this category would include having regular science lessons, making observations and performing experiments, opportunity to learn, and length and extent of science instruction. One notion implied in this group of variables is that if science is going to be learned by students, it is going to be learned largely in school. Providing for such learning would appear to be critical. In Literature, the case is less clear. At Population II, two variables that are indicators of teacher quality entered the regression analysis with modest contribu-

---

[2] One explanation for the larger variation in Science for Population IV is that schools vary fairly widely in the number of years of science their students have studied. Simply put, if schools don't teach science, students don't learn it. Although this is a likely explanation for Science, it does not hold for Literature.

tions. They were not in evidence at Population IV, however. Thus, there is little specific guidance to offer on literature instruction.

The independent contribution of the kindred variables is interesting but may not be practically useful. Variables that serve as indicators of attitudes, habits, and interests are consistently related to achievement in all three subjects. Hours of reading for pleasure per week, paucity of television viewing, reading resources, favorable attitudes, and parental interest in the students' progress in school are variables reflecting these concomitants of achievement. The unexpected finding that an interest in reading humorous books and the comics section of the newspaper is related to achievement in reading and literature warrants further study.

Chapter 8

Between-Student Differences
in Achievement

This chapter presents the results of the between-student regression analyses for Science, Reading Comprehension, Literature, Civic Education, and French Reading and Listening Comprehension. The individual student serves as the basic unit of analysis; attention is focused on the correlates of student achievement. Teacher variables within a school have been averaged; these values are assigned to each individual student in the school. Similarly, the value of each school variable has been assigned to all members of that school's sample.

The level of relationship between various predictor variables and school achievement is in all cases decidedly lower than that reported for between-school differences in achievement. The ecological correlations reported in the previous chapter used the average of student performance to characterize the achievement of the school. Individual student differences in performance are thus effectively eliminated and neighborhood effects accentuated. In the results reported here, differences between individual students constitute the basis of the analyses.

Results are presented for each population level in each subject area. Background variables are entered first, followed by community type and program placement, learning conditions, and finally the kindred variables. In the French testing, an additional block has been added before the learning conditions. This block is titled Time Factors and includes the student's age, grade placement, and number of years of French study. It was felt that in foreign language learning time was such a critical factor that variables indicative of it should be grouped into a special block. In each table of results, the simple correlation of each variable with the criterion is reported, along with the weight (standardized regression coefficient) it has in the full regression equation, and its unique contribution to the final R^2, i. e., the increase in the value of R^2 that would be obtained if the variable had been entered last in the regression analysis. Lastly, the value of the multiple correlation, R, and the proportion of variance in the achievement test scores, R^2, are reported for each block.

SCIENCE

The results of the regression analyses for Science for Populations I, II, and IV are presented in Tables 58, 59, and 60, respectively. At Population I, slightly over one-third of the variance in Science achievement test scores ($R^2 = .34$) is accounted for by the twenty variables included in the analysis. 18% of the variation is accounted for by the background variables alone, the notable contributor being the School Handicap Score. The unique contribution of the School Handicap Score is .056, however, indicating that it shares a considerable amount of variance with other predictor variables.

The learning condition variables collectively account for 9% of the variance in the achievement test scores. Of the ten variables in this block, the one with the highest simple correlation with achievement is grade, which is more properly viewed as a placement variable indicating previous learning rather than as a condition of present learning. Three variables relating to science instruction that have moderate simple correlation with achievement are observing and experimenting during science lessons, use of a science textbook, and having regular science lessons. Collectively, these variables can be viewed as indicators of a deliberate instructional effort in science. The variable that appears as an anomaly is students' designing their own experiments. This variable shows both a negative simple correlation with achievement ($r = -.12$) and a negative regression weight. That is, students who respond positively to the item perform less well on the Science tests than do students who respond negatively. It would appear that such activity is negatively related to achievement since it may reflect a "messing around" approach in contrast to a more structured approach to the learning of science.

The kindred variables account for an additional 7% of the variation in Science achievement scores. Of the variables in this block, scores on the School Motivation Scale have the highest simple correlation with achievement ($r = .34$), as well as the largest weight. The number of hours per week spent reading for pleasure is the next most prominent variable in this block. The Like School Scale has a somewhat surprisingly low correlation with achievement ($r = .04$), and the amount of TV viewing has an expected negative correlation with Science achievement test scores ($r = -.11$).

The results for Population II are quite similar to those for Population I. Slightly over one-third of the total variance of achievement test scores is accounted for by the variables included in the analysis. The background variables account for 21% of the total variation in achievement at Population II, in contrast to 18% at Population I. The School Handicap Score is again the most prominent predictor. Type of program in which the student is enrolled, however, enters into the regression equation because of the differentiation that typically occurs at the secondary school level. The thirteen learning condition variables account for 6% of the variation in achievement test scores. Of the variables in this block, grade, number of hours of homework per week, currently taking a science course, and total amount of science studied have the highest simple correlations with achievement. Only the grade in which the student is enrolled, however, has a sizable weight. The remaining variables in the block have very small regression weights and make such small unique contributions to the overall R^2 that not much attention should be accorded them.

The three kindred variables account for an additional 6% of the variation in Science achievement test scores. Each variable has a moderate correlation with achievement, ranging from $r = .35$ for scores on the Science Interest Scale to $r = .20$ for the number of hours per week spent reading for pleasure.

The results for Population IV are strikingly similar to those for the earlier population levels. The twenty variables that are included in the analysis account for 39% of the variance in Science achievement test scores. The background variables account for 18% of the variation, precisely the same amount as at Population I. The School Handicap Score is again the most prominent predictor with a simple correlation of .30, down from .40 obtained at Populations I and II. This is probably due to the fact that schooling is no longer compulsory at this level and, consequently, there is some restriction in range because of dropouts.

The correlation between sex and Science achievement is now $-.28$, compared with $-.09$ and $-.22$ at Populations I and II, respectively. Since boys were coded as "1" and girls as "2" for the analysis, the negative sign of the correlation indicates that boys perform higher on the Science achievement tests than do girls. The increasing magnitude of the relationship between sex and achievement from Population I to IV indicates that the difference between the sexes increases with additional schooling. This may be a reflection of socialization processes.

An additional 9% of the variance in Science achievement test scores is accounted for by the variables in the second block. The important variable here is the type of program in which the student is

Table 58

Results of the Between-Student Regression Analysis for Science at Population I

Block and Variable	r	Wt.	Unique Contri- bution to R²	R	R²
I Background					
School Handicap Score	.40	.26	.056		
Daily newspaper in home	.17	.05	.002		
Sex of student	-.09	-.14	.019		
Age	-.00	-.04	.001	.42	.18
II Type of community/program					
Type of community	.16	.08	.006	.43	.18
III Learning conditions					
Grade	.19	.16	.018		
Design own experiments	-.17	-.14	.018		
Observe and experiment	.18	.08	.006		
Use of textbook	.17	.07	.005		
Total enrollment	-.06	-.07	.005		
Opportunity to learn	.06	.06	.003		
Regular science lessons	.12	.04	.002		
Percent male teachers	.05	.04	.002		
Pupil/teacher ratio	.01	.04	.002		
Class size	-.03	-.02	.001	.52	.27

IV Kindreds			
School motivation	.34	.25	.046
Hours reading for pleasure per week	.23	.11	.012
Like School Scale	.04	-.07	.004
Hours T.V. per day	-.11	-.05	.002
Parents help with homework	-.06	-.03	.001
		Total	.211 .59 .34

Table 59

Results of the Between-Student Regression Analysis for Science at Population II

Block and Variable	r	Wt.	Unique Contribution to R^2	R	R^2
I Background					
School Handicap Score	.40	.24	.044		
Sex of student	-.22	-.18	.029	.45	.21
II Type of community/program					
Type of community	.24	.08	.006		
Type of program	.12	.08	.005	.49	.24
III Learning Conditions					
Grade	.19	.19	.030		
Taking science	.14	.09	.007		
Hours homework per week	.19	.04	.001		
Percent male teachers	.11	.07	.003		
Teachers post-secondary school training	.08	.05	.002		
Total amount of science studied	.15	.03	.001		
Community resources	-.06	-.07	.004		
Percent of teachers teaching science	.04	.03	.001		
Admission based on performance	.08	.04	.002		

Visitations by outside authorities for reporting purposes	.02	.02	.000		
Practical work in science	.03	.03	.001		
Lab assistants in science	-.04	-.04	.001		
Subject matter association member	.01	-.02	.000	.55	.30
IV Kindreds					
Science interest scale	.35	.20	.032		
Hours reading for pleasure per week	.20	.09	.007		
Expected amount of further education	.28	.10	.007		
Total			.183	.60	.36

Table 60

Results of the Between-Student Regression Analysis for Science at Population IV

Block and Variable	r	Wt.	Unique Contri-bution to R^2	R	R^2
I Background					
School Handicap Score	.30	.13	.014		
Sex of student	-.28	-.20	.034		
Age	-.13	-.07	.004	.43	.18
II Type of community/program					
Type of program	.41	.19	.023		
Type of community	-.04	.10	.006	.52	.27
III Learning conditions					
Science study and homework	.38	.13	.013		
Years of science study	.35	.11	.009		
Percent male teachers in school	.04	.07	.003		
Use of printed drill material	-.01	-.07	.004		
Students involved in decision making	-.05	-.07	.004		
Inspection of school by outside authorities	-.08	-.05	.002		

Total enrollment of school	.06	.09	.004		
Opportunity to learn material on test	-.03	-.05	.002		
Grade	.02	.03	.001		
Percent time teachers are employed	.04	.04	.001		
Sex of teachers	-.04	-.06	.002		
Ancillary staff	-.03	-.06	.002	.59	.35
IV Kindreds					
Science attitude scale	.43	.20	.029		
Hours reading for pleasure per week	.18	.06	.004		
Expected occupational level	.14	.03	.001		
Total			.162	.63	.39

enrolled. Students enrolled in academic programs perform substantially better than do students enrolled in general programs. Students enrolled in vocational programs performed at the lowest levels on the test.

Twelve learning condition variables account for an additional 8% of the variation in Science achievement test scores. Of these, only two have sizable simple correlations with achievement—science study and homework, and years of science study. Both are more accurately viewed as measures of previous learning conditions than of present ones. The remaining variables have rather low simple correlations with achievement as well as low regression weights, and it would seem wise to pay little heed to them.

Three kindred variables entered into the regression equation. The Science Attitude Scale shows an appreciable correlation with achievement and has a sizable regression weight. Number of hours of pleasure reading is again included. The status level of the students' expected future occupation shows a rather modest relationship with achievement and has a low regression weight, probably due in part to some restriction of range at this level and perhaps to the lack of crystallization of occupational interests.

READING COMPREHENSION

Tables 61, 62, and 63 present the results of the between-student regression analyses for Populations I, II, and IV, respectively. A slightly different procedure was adopted for estimating home influences here so that no School Handicap Score is reported. Instead, a home background composite, which comprised the same variables used in the School Handicap Score, was computed for Populations II and IV. The weights given to different categories of response for each variable differed somewhat from those used in computing the School Handicap Score, however. At Population I, the criterion-scaled variable representing the status level of the father's occupation, the major component of the School Handicap Score, was entered singly. The results for all three population levels are strikingly similar. The background factors account for 20%, 22%, and 17% of the variance in the test scores at Populations I, II, and IV, respectively. Sex differences are negligible at Population I but increase slightly with increases in age and grade. Girls perform slightly better than boys at all levels.

The second block of variables shows an increasing influence with increasing age and grade. This reflects the importance of the type of program in which the student is enrolled. At Population IV, in fact, type of program is the single best predictor of student achievement and is accorded the highest weight.

The learning condition variables account for very small proportions of additional variance in Reading Comprehension test scores at all levels. Grade appears to be important at Populations I and II, whereas the number of hours of homework the student reports doing each week is important at Populations II and IV. Results for these two variables are highly consistent. At first glance, it would appear that hours of homework may offer promise as a malleable instructional variable. Such an interpretation, however, may not be justified. Increasing the amount of homework assigned to students who are not performing well in school may simply result in their refusal to do it. Since the amount of additional variance accounted for by the other variables in the third block is so low and the simple correlations are uniformly low, it would seem better to disregard them.

The kindred variables account for 6% additional variance at Populations I and IV and 11% at Population II. The number of hours of pleasure reading is included at all three levels as an important concomitant of Reading Comprehension. Other important kindreds of achievement are scores on the School Motivation Scale at Population I, current types of books being read and additional amount of education expected at Population II, and current types of books being read, status of expected occupational level, and scores on the Literary Interest Scale at Population IV. Parental help with homework shows an increasingly negative correlation from Population I to II, indicating that students who are in greater need of help with their homework, due to low achievement, are receiving it.

The overall regression results in Reading Comprehension are somewhat unimpressive. Between 31% and 42% of the variation in Reading Comprehension test scores is accounted for by the total set of predictor variables. It would seem that either survey methods that do not include some direct measure of the capabilities of the individual student are not adequate to the task of isolating the determinants of individual achievement or that the critical variables have not as yet been identified. Both explanations, of course, can hold.

LITERATURE

The results of the regression analyses for Literature for Populations II and IV are presented in Tables 64 and 65.[1] The results for both

---

[1] Only Populations II and IV were tested in this subject because of the low emphasis given to the study of literature at the elementary school level.

Table 61

Results of the Between-Student Regression Analysis for Reading
Comprehension at Population I

Block and Variable	r	Wt.	Unique Contribution to R^2	R	R^2
I Background					
Father's occupation	.37	.23	.046		
Reading resources in the home	.29	.13	.014		
Number of siblings	-.17	.10	.009		
Sex of student	.07	.01	.000		
Age	.01	-.04	.001	.44	.20
II Type of community/program					
Type of community	.19	.08	.006	.46	.21
III Learning conditions					
Grade	.22	.18	.025		
Teacher aides	-.11	.06	.003		
Years principal has been at school	-.03	-.03	.001		
PTA--raises money	-.01	-.04	.001		
PTA--parent education	-.01	.03	.000	.50	.25

IV Kindreds			
School motivation scale	.32	.18	.026
Hours reading for pleasure per week	.28	.15	.021
Parents help with homework	-.07	-.05	.003
Hours of T.V. watched per day	-.10	-.04	.002
Like School Scale	.08	-.03	.001
			Total .159 .56 .31

Table 62

Results of the Between-Student Regression Analysis for Reading
Comprehension at Population II

Block and Variable	r	wt.	Unique Contri-bution to R^2	R	R^2
I Background					
Home background	.42	.20	.030		
Reading resources in the home	.33	.09	.006		
Number of siblings	-.12	-.07	.005		
Age	.02	-.04	.001	.47	.22
II Type of community/program					
Type of program	.32	.15	.017		
Type of community	.10	.05	.001	.51	.26
III Learning conditions					
Grade	.25	.18	.022		
Hours of homework per week	.25	.05	.002		
Grouping for reading in the classroom	-.09	-.05	.002		

Age of teacher	.13	.03	.001		
Sex of teacher	−.05	−.03	.001		
Size of English class	.06	.03	.001		
Location of community	−.07	−.06	.003		
Within class grouping	−.08	−.02	.000		
Pupil/teacher ratio	−.05	−.01	.000	.57	.32
IV Kindreds					
Hours reading for pleasure per week	.36	.17	.023		
Parents help with homework	−.20	−.15	.022		
Movie attendance	−.18	−.14	.018		
Current reading of books	.24	.09	.007		
Read news and comic section of newspaper	.19	.08	.005		
Expected amount of further education	.26	.08	.005		
Hours of T.V. viewing and radio listening	.10	.06	.004		
School motivation scale	.08	−.04	.001		
Watch T.V. documentaries	.05	.02	.000		
		Total	.177	.65	.43

Table 63

Results of the Between-Student Regression Analysis for Reading Comprehension at Population IV

Block and Variable	r	Wt.	Unique Contribution to R²	R	R²
I Background					
Home background	.34	.16	.019		
Reading resources in home	.29	.09	.005		
Age	-.19	-.13	.014		
Number of siblings	-.09	-.02	.001		
Sex of student	.08	.00	.000		
				.42	.17
II Type of community/program					
Type of program	.41	.24	.042		
Type of community	.07	.09	.008		
				.51	.26
III Learning conditions					
Hours of homework per week	.25	.08	.005		
Importance of examinations	-.07	-.08	.006		
Visitations by outside authorities for reporting purposes	.03	.09	.008		
Amount of teachers' post-secondary schooling	.08	.08	.006		
Total enrollment of school	.10	.05	.002		
				.53	.28

IV	Kindreds			
	Hours reading for pleasure per week	.27	.10	.008
	Current reading	.29	.10	.007
	Parents correct speaking and writing	.03	-.09	.007
	Current newspaper read	.16	.07	.004
	Expected occupational level	.20	.05	.002
	Amount of T.V. viewing	.10	.05	.002
	Like school scale	.17	.03	.001
	Literary interest scale	.20	.03	.001
	Total	.58	.34	.148

Table 64

Results of the Between-Student Regression Analysis for
Literature at Population II

Block and Variable	r	Wt.	Unique Contri-bution to R^2	R	R^2
I Background					
Home background	.32	.11	.009		
Sex of student	.22	.19	.018		
Reading resources in home	.26	.04	.002		
Number of siblings	-.12	-.07	.000		
				.43	.19
II Type of community/program					
Type of program	.25	.10	.009		
Type of community	.08	.04	.001		
				.46	.21
III Learning conditions					
Recite literary passages					
from memory	-.17	-.12	.013		
Hours homework per week	.24	.06	.003		
Grade	.20	.10	.000		
Methods-textbook	.11	.04	.001		
Prop. of class time devoted					
to literature	.15	.08	.005		
Write about literature	.13	.04	.001		
Sex of teacher	-.04	-.05	.002		
Public library available	.09	.06	.003		
Hours of homework in					
literature	.07	-.06	.003		
Class size in literature	.07	.03	.001		
Percent of teachers male	-.07	-.03	.001		
Age of teachers	.07	.03	.001		
Admission based on performance	.12	.03	.001		
Pupil/teacher ratio	-.06	-.02	.000		
				.53	.29
IV Kindreds					
Hours reading for pleasure					
per week	.33	.13	.014		
Current reading	.27	.15	.017		
Attendance at movies	-.14	-.12	.013		
Newspaper reading	.21	.10	.008		
Watch T.V. dramas	.19	.09	.007		
Other current reading	.10	-.09	.005		
Expected amount of further					
education	.21	.09	.006		
Hours of T.V. viewing and					
radio listening	.08	.07	.005		
Read about sports	-.17	-.07	.003		
		Total .155		.61	.38

Table 65

Results of the Between-Student Regression Analysis for
Literature at Population IV

Block and Variable	r	Wt.	Unique Contri-bution to R^2	R	R^2
I Background					
Home background	.27	.11	.009		
Sex of student	.23	.13	.011		
Reading resources in the home	.24	.04	.001		
Age	-.22	-.13	.015		
				.40	.16
II Type of community/program					
Type of program	.29	.13	.011		
Type of community	.02	-.01	.000		
				.44	.20
III Learning conditions					
Proportion of class time					
devoted to literature	.26	.13	.015		
Teacher's impression of students'					
interest in literature	.12	.11	.010		
Enrollment	.11	.13	.012		
Educational and cultural					
amenities in community	-.00	-.09	.003		
Hours spent marking papers per					
week	.06	-.10	.007		
Teachers' total amount of					
education	.08	.07	.005		
Public library available	-.03	.05	.001		
Sex of teacher	-.01	.03	.001		
Grade	.05	.03	.001		
				.50	.25
IV Kindreds					
Current reading	.28	.12	.001		
Other newspaper reading	-.02	-.14	.017		
Literary interest scale	.24	.11	.008		
Hours spent reading for					
pleasure per week	.25	.09	.005		
Expected occupational level	.20	.05	.002		
Parents encourage visits to					
museums	.07	-.04	.001		
Like school scale	.13	-.04	.001		
Amount of further education					
expected	.18	.04	.001		
Current newspaper read	.18	.03	.001		
			Total .139	.55	.31

populations are quite similar when one takes into account the fact that schooling is no longer compulsory at Population IV. 37% of the variance in Literature test scores is accounted for by the predictor variables at Population II, and 30% at Population IV. 19% of the total variation is accounted for by the background variables at Population II, in contrast to 16% at Population IV. At both levels, the variable in this block that is most closely related to achievement is the home background composite. In contrast to Reading Comprehension, sex of the student shows a substantially greater correlation with achievement—$r = .22$ at Population II and $.23$ at Population IV. These positive correlations indicate that the girls outperform the boys. At both population levels, the reading resources in the home, i. e., sheer number of books, possession of a dictionary and an encyclopedia, are associated with higher levels of achievement.

The type of program in which the student is enrolled again makes a difference. The simple correlations between type of program and Literature achievement are .25 and .29 for Populations II and IV, respectively. There are a substantial number of learning condition variables in the regression equation at each level, but they account for only 8% and 5% additional variance in Literature test performance at Populations II and IV, respectively. Since literature is typically taught in an English class, it is not surprising that variables associated with the amount of time spent on literature activities are associated with Literature achievement. Providing time and opportunity to study literature appear to be clearly related to performance. Hours of homework per week is also related to performance at Population II but, somewhat surprisingly, is not included at Population IV. The majority of the variables in this block, however, have small and often not readily explainable relationships with achievement. In one case, availability of a public library, the sign of the simple correlation with achievement changes from one level to another. It would seem best to ignore these variables rather than to attempt to concoct an explanation for them.

The kindred variables account for an additional 9% and 6% of the variation in achievement test performance at Populations II and IV, respectively. The variables in this block, indicative of reading habits, interests, and activities, show a moderate relationship with achievement. At both population levels, the amount of pleasure reading shows the highest relationship with Literature test performance. Other indicators of the amount or type of reading activity show only slightly lower relationships with test performance.

CIVIC EDUCATION

The regression analysis results for Civic Education are presented in Tables 66 and 67 for Populations II and IV, respectively. As in the case of Literature, there is a striking similarity in the results at the two levels. The background variables account for 20% of the variance in Civic Education achievement test scores at Population II, and 18% at Population IV. The School Handicap Score is the variable that has the highest simple correlation with achievement at both levels. The sex of students is negatively related to achievement, indicating higher performance for boys than for girls. At Population II, the difference between the sexes is slight ($r = -.04$), but it increases at Population IV ($r = -.15$). This perhaps reflects the effect of socialization processes.

The negative correlations between number of siblings and achievement indicate that students from smaller families perform better on the Civic Education test than do students from larger families. Since family size and social class are known to be related, however, the negative simple correlations with achievement probably include the confounding effect of social class. The regression weight and the unique contribution to R^2 of the number of siblings both have low values. Thus, although there is an independent relationship of number of siblings with achievement, it is lower than indicated by the simple correlation.

In the second block, the type of program in which the student is enrolled is substantially related to Civic Education achievement, the correlations being .40 and .43 at Populations II and IV, respectively. Again, this placement variable is indicative more of the students' previous learning than anything else. The socioeconomic status of the community in which the student resides also contributes modestly to the explanation of variations in achievement test performance.

The learning condition variables account for a rather disappointing 3% or 4% of the variation in Civic Education test performance. It may be that, like Reading Comprehension, achievement in Civic Education is the result more of out-of-school factors than of direct instruction. Because of the small amount of variation accounted for by variables in this block and the typically low simple correlations of the variables with the criterion, little attention will be given to these variables. There are, however, several variables of special interest. Carrying out patriotic rituals in the classroom is associated with lower levels of achievement at both population levels. Encouraging students to be independent in the classroom is modestly but positively as-

Table 66

Results of the Between-Student Regression Analysis for Civic
Education at Population II

Block and Variable	r	Wt.	Unique Contribution to R²	R	R²
I Background					
School Handicap Score	.44	.23	.038		
Number of siblings	-.11	-.05	.002		
Sex of student	-.04	-.08	.005	.45	.20
II Type of community/program					
Type of program	.40	.22	.040		
Community socioeconomic status	.12	.05	.003	.52	.27
III Learning Conditions					
Non-political good citizenship	.03	.10	.003		
Patriotic rituals in the classroom	-.11	-.09	.008		
Independence encouraged in classroom	.11	.02	.005		
Frequency of within-class grouping	-.03	-.03	.001		
Frequency of use of audio-visual aids	.08	.08	.005		
Hours spent in preparing lessons	-.04	-.06	.003		
Grade in which social studies courses begin	.04	-.03	.001		

	.10	.03	.001	.55	.30
Tolerance for discussion of issues in the classroom					
IV Kindreds					
Hours of reading for pleasure each week	.32	.19	.029		
Expected number of years of further education	.40	.17	.021		
Voting in peer group	.20	.10	.009		
Interest in watching civic affairs program on T.V.	.21	.09	.006		
Anticipatory socialization	-.11	-.05	.002		
Parent involvement with child's education	.14	-.05	.002		
Discuss civic education matters with friends	.03	.04	.002		
Like school scale score	.25	.04	.001		
School not located in a rural area	.08	-.03	.001		
Total			.193	.63	.40

Table 67

Results of the Between-Student Regression Analysis for Civic Education at Population IV

Block and Variable	r	Wt.	Unique contri-bution to R^2	R	R^2
I Background					
School Handicap Score	.39	.19	.025		
Dictionary in home	.10	.01	.000		
Number of siblings	-.14	-.08	.006		
Sex of student	-.10	-.08	.005		
Age	-.15	-.07	.005		
II Type of community/program				.43	.18
Student's program	.43	.24	.044		
Community socioeconomic status	.16	.07	.004		
III Learning conditions				.52	.27
Patriotic rituals in the classroom	-.17	-.08	.005		
Teacher's amount of post-secondary school education	.13	.09	.007		
Factual knowledge stressed in civic ed. classes	-.14	-.08	.006		
Frequency of assessment of student performance on projects	.11	.03	.001		
Sex of teacher	-.04	-.07	.004		
Amount of in-service training in subject matter	-.05	-.07	.003		
Frequency of use of drill material	-.04	.04	.001		
Frequency of use of standardized tests to assess students	-.09	-.03	.001		

Hours spent in preparing lessons	.06	.05	.001	
Non-political good citizenship	-.01	.05	.002	
Admissions criteria--use of an examination	.04	-.05	.002	
Grade in which social studies courses begin	.09	.04	.001	
Importance of teaching about non-western cultures	.10	.02	.000	
Independence encouraged in classroom	-.03	-.05	.002	
Teaching in area of specialization	.15	.04	.001	
Amount of pre-service education in the social sciences	.01	-.02	.000	.56 .31
IV Kindreds				
Hours of reading for pleasure per week	.29	.18	.027	
Amount of further education expected	.35	.11	.009	
Interest in watching civic affairs programs on T.V.	.14	.07	.005	
Parent involvement with child's education	.11	-.08	.005	
Amount of discussion of civic affairs with others	.18	.07	.004	
Voting in peer group	.07	.06	.004	
School not located in a rural area	.07	-.04	.001	
Total			.181	.62 .38

sociated with achievement at Population II ($r = .11$), but shows almost no relationship with achievement at Population IV ($r = -.03$). On the other hand, stress on acquiring a fund of factual knowledge is negatively related to achievement at Population IV ($r = -.14$).

The kindred variables account for an additional 7% and 10% of the variation in achievement at Populations II and IV, respectively. The variable in this block with the highest simple correlation with achievement at both levels is the amount of further schooling that the student expects. Why this variable should emerge so clearly in Civic Education and not in any other subject is not completely clear. Perhaps students who score high on the Civic Education test also have a keener sense of the relationship between education and advancement in our society and consequently expect to complete more years of additional schooling in order to increase their chances of securing economic, social, and cultural rewards.

The second most prominent variable among the list of kindreds is the amount of reading for pleasure. The emergence of this variable once again with its substantial regression weight as well as its moderate correlation with achievement marks it as the most consistent concomitant of achievement. Deciding issues among peers by voting is related to Civic Education achievement, although the simple correlations differ somewhat at the two population levels. It would appear that practicing democratic procedures tends to be associated with higher levels of achievement but this may also be due to confounding with other variables, notably socio-economic status.

A third variable that shows a modest but consistent positive relationship with achievement is the student's reported interest in watching civic affairs programs on television. Also, at Population IV, the student's reported discussion of civic affairs with others is associated with higher levels of achievement ($r = .18$). Lastly, at Population II, scores on the scale indicating a liking for school are positively associated with Civic Education achievement ($r = .25$).

The total amount of explained variation in Civic Education test performance is virtually the same at both levels (.38 and .40). The unexplained variance is, however, considerable. It would seem that many important determiners of achievement in civic education have not been measured or have been measured inadequately. The inclusion of a number of malleable variables in the block denoting learning conditions, albeit with low simple correlations, may suggest promising variables for further, more detailed studies.

FRENCH READING

The results of the regression analyses for French Reading Comprehension are presented in Tables 68 and 69. The tables differ somewhat from those previously presented. The inclusion of a new block, time factors, reflects the importance of the number of years of study of a foreign language on achievement. The block is placed third in order of entry, after the general placement variables and before the learning condition variables. This form of organization is repeated for French Listening Comprehension results.

The overall results for French Reading appear to be somewhat disappointing, especially at Population II, where the multiple correlation ($R = .47$) is lower than for any other subject at any population level. There are two reasons for this. First, French is an optional subject in the school curriculum and many students never study it. In contrast, virtually every student studies science, reading, literature, and social studies at some point in his or her school career. Curtailment of variability due to the optional nature of the subject can serve to reduce the level of relationship between achievement in French and the various predictor variables. Second, students at the Population II level have usually only recently begun their study of French (52% of the students are in their first year of French and another 20% are in their second year). The United States mean for years of study is substantially lower than that of any other country. A consequence of this is that the variability in achievement is lower than for groups that have studied French for a longer period. The U.S. standard deviation in French reading is the lowest among all participating countries at this level. Again, curtailment of variability operates to reduce the level of obtained relationships between French achievement and various predictors.

The phenomena described above are illustrated in the results for the block of background variables. The simple correlations between the School Handicap Score and French Reading achievement are .14 and .17 at Populations II and IV, respectively. This is lower than for any other subject at any level and reflects the fact that a rather homogeneous group of students elects to study French. The small positive correlations between sex and achievement indicate that girls outperform boys in French Reading, but the difference is slight. At Population IV, there is a unique independent contribution of the socioeconomic status of the community in explaining variation in

Table 68

Results of the Between-Student Regression Analysis for French Reading at Population II

Block and Variable	r	Wt.	Unique contribution to R²	R	R²
I Background					
School Handicap Score	.14	.08	.006		
Sex of student	.08	.08	.005	.16	.03
II Type of school/program					
Type of program	.11	.04	.002	.18	.03
III Time factors					
Years studied French	.21	.17	.027		
Age	-.05	-.02	.000	.27	.08
IV Learning conditions					
Methods of teaching grammar	.18	.15	.020		
Frequency of doing French translation in class	.15	.10	.006		
Number of French teachers	.14	.14	.014		
Years teaching foreign language	.04	.07	.004		
Teacher's perceived skill in writing French	.00	-.09	.003		
Use of an admissions examination	-.00	-.09	.004		
Coeducation at Population II	-.04	-.04	.001		
Total instructional time in French at beginning level	-.01	.01	.000		
Teacher's perceived ability to speak French	.04	.08	.002		
Teacher lived in a French-speaking country	.02	-.04	.001		
Frequency of speaking in English in French class	-.01	.01	.000		
Amount of post-high school French	-.01	-.03	.001		
Sex of teacher	-.02	.02	.000		
Amount of French writing done in class	.10	.00	.000	.39	.15

V Kindreds			
Aspiration to read French	.26	.07	.002
Difficulty in learning French as compared with other subjects	.22	.10	.008
Total activities in French in school	.15	.06	.003
Parents help with homework	.06	.08	.007
Interest in French scale	.24	.04	.001
Time spent visiting in a French-speaking country	.10	.05	.002
Aspiration to understand spoken French	.25	.06	.001
Hours of homework per week	.11	.03	.001
Perceived utility of learning French	.20	.04	.001
Total	.122	.47	.22

Table 69

Results of the Between-Student Regression Analysis for French Reading at Population IV

Block and Variable	r	Wt.	Unique contribution to R2	R	R2
I Background					
School Handicap Score	.17	.08	.005		
Sex of student	.05	.02	.000		
Socioeconomic status of community	.15	.21	.030	.23	.05
II Type of school/program					
Type of program	.12	.01	.000	.24	.06
III Time Factors					
Grade	.19	.18	.019		
Years studied French	.22	.06	.003		
Age	.10	-.06	.002	.36	.13
IV Learning conditions					
Number of French teachers in school	.24	.18	.026		
Frequency of speaking French to the teacher	.19	.07	.003		
Frequency of speaking English in French class	-.25	-.08	.004		
Teacher's perceived listening ability in French	.19	.08	.004		
Number of years of foreign language teaching	.06	.05	.002		
Frequency of translation work in French class	-.12	-.08	.005		
Teacher's perceived writing ability in French	.08	-.06	.002		
Sex of teachers	.18	.07	.002		
Methods of teaching grammar in French	-.04	-.03	.001		
Years of post-secondary study of French	.03	-.02	.000		
Teacher's perceived ability to speak French	.10	.02	.000	.51	.26

V Kindreds

Aspiration to read French	.43	.14	.007
Difficulty in learning French as compared to other subjects	.28	.13	.014
Perceived utility of learning French	.33	.06	.002
Parents help with homework	.11	.08	.005
Parents interest in school	.13	-.09	.004
Aspiration to speak French	.42	.05	.005
Amount of additional education expected	.08	.05	.002
Hours of homework per week	.13	.04	.001
Interest in French scale	.35	.05	.001
Aspiration to understand spoken French	.42	.04	.001
Total activities in French in school	.23	.02	.000
Total	.62	.39	.150

student achievement. Higher achievement is associated with living in a community where the average years of education of adults and the average family income level are high. The results for the block of variables, however, are unimpressive. At Population II, the background factors account for a meager 3% of the variance in French Reading achievement test scores, and only 5% at Population IV.

The type of program in which the student is enrolled also shows a low relationship with achievement and contributes little to the prediction of French Reading achievement. This is due simply to the fact that the bulk of the students who are studying French report that they are enrolled in an academic program. With little variability, the correlation cannot be high.

The third block of variables, time factors, shows somewhat higher correlations. The number of years of French study is among the best predictors of French reading achievement. It too is depressed, however, because of lack of variability. Nevertheless, the variables in this block account for an additional 5% and 7% of the variation in French Reading achievement, an amount greater than that accounted for by the background variables in the first block.

A considerable number of variables enter into the regression analyses at block four, the learning condition variables, and account for an additional 7% and 13% of the variance in French Reading achievement at Populations II and IV, respectively. Although these amounts are not startlingly high, they are considerably higher than the amount accounted for by the background variables and, when combined with the time factors of the third block, account for over one-half of the explained variance in achievement. At both population levels, the variables fall into two broad groups, although the simple correlations with achievement are modest. One group of variables is associated with teacher competence in French. Thus, schools that have a sizable group of French teachers who have had considerable formal training and teaching experience, have lived in a French-speaking country, and perceive themselves as being proficient in French, have higher performing students than do schools with less qualified teachers. Collectively they appear to define an important dimension that is related to student achievement.

A second group of variables may be termed instructional procedures; this includes methods of teaching grammar (an eclectic approach vs. a highly formal or an inductive approach), carrying out French translations in class, using French as a medium of instruction, and writing in French. Again, the simple correlations of these variables with French achievement are generally modest but, taken together, serve to define an approach to the teaching of French that is associated with higher levels of achievement. This approach is highly task oriented and designed to blanket the students in a range of French learning activities. The combination of teacher competence and the instructional procedures accounts for a considerable amount of the explained variation in the French Reading achievement of students even when background factors and type of program have been accounted for.

The kindred variables furnish an interesting picture of the concomitants of French Reading achievement. The variables included in this block are virtually identical for both population levels and account for an additional 7% and 13% of the variation in student achievement at Populations II and IV, respectively. Interestingly, these are the same amounts accounted for by the learning condition variables. The variable in this block that has the highest simple correlation with French achievement at both levels is the student's reported aspiration to be able to read French. In fact, the variable correlates higher with French Reading achievement than does any other variable at either population level. Higher aspiration is clearly associated with higher achievement. A second important concomitant is the student's aspiration to understand spoken French. It is the variable that has the next highest relationship with the criterion. These variables, along with most of the others in the block, are indicative of student interest, attitude, and commitment to learning French. It would appear that they reflect a level of dedication to learning French that is critical for success

When one compares the results of the regression analyses for French Reading achievement with the results for the other subjects, the predictors are not consistent. At Population II, less of the variation in achievement has been accounted for by the predictor variables than anywhere else, whereas at Population IV the overall amount of variation accounted for is just about the same as in other subjects. Reasons for these discrepancies at Population II have already been cited. The learning condition variables, however, reflect a set of instructional procedures that are highly malleable and suggest ways of teaching French reading that appear promising. It is hoped that educators concerned with French teaching and learning will study them further and in more detail than could be done in the present investiga tion.

FRENCH LISTENING

The results for French Listening Comprehension are roughly similar to those for French Reading. They are presented in Tables 70 and 71 for

Table 70

Results of the Between-Student Regression Analysis for
French Listening at Population II

	Block and Variable	r	Wt.	Unique Contri- bution to R²	R	R²
I	Background					
	School Handicap Score	.15	.11	.009		
	Socioeconomic status of community	-.05	-.06	.003	.17	.03
II	Type of school/program					
	Type of program	.08	.04	.002	.17	.03
III	Time Factors					
	Years studied French	.27	.18	.013		
	Grade in which French study began	-.24	-.08	.003	.31	.10
IV	Learning conditions					
	Hours spent marking papers	.12	.07	.005		
	Frequency of speaking in French to the teacher	.07	.01	.000		
	Methods of teaching grammar in French	.09	.12	.014		
	Years teaching foreign languages	.08	.13	.014		
	Use of an admissions examination	-.10	-.11	.005		
	Coeducation at Population II	-.03	-.13	.010		
	Teacher's perceived listening ability in French	.10	.09	.005		
	Teacher's perceived pronunciation skill in French	-.03	-.14	.011		
	Teacher's perceived skill in reading French	.13	.10	.005		
	Total instructional time for beginning French	.03	.05	.002		
	Teacher lived in French-speaking country	-.00	-.10	.006		
	Teacher's perceived skill in speaking French	.09	.14	.007		
	Number of French teachers in the school	.01	.06	.002		

Speaking in English in French class	-.03	-.04	.001	
Writing in English in French class	.07	.04	.001	
Teacher's perceived skill in writing French	.07	-.06	.002	
Classes conducted in French in Grades 1-8	.02	-.04	.001	
Emphasis on translation in French class	.03	-.05	.001	.43
				.19
V Kindreds				
Difficulty in learning French as compared with other subjects	.24	.13	.014	
Total activities in French in school	.22	.13	.015	
Aspiration to understand spoken French	.23	.08	.002	
Time spent visiting in a French-speaking country	.01	-.06	.003	
Parents help with homework	.03	.04	.002	
Interest in French scale	.22	.05	.001	
Parent's interest in school	.08	-.07	.003	
Hours of homework per week	.04	-.04	.001	
Perceived utility of learning French	.20	.05	.001	
Aspiration to read French	.22	.05	.001	
Aspiration to write French	.19	-.04	.001	.52
				.27
Total			.166	

Table 71

Results of the Between-Student Regression Analysis for
French Listening at Population IV

Block and Variable	r	Wt.	Unique Contribution to R²	R	R²
I Background					
School Handicap Score	.19	.06	.003	.19	.04
II Type of school/program					
Type of program	.17	-.04	.001	.23	.05
III Time factors					
Years studied French	.42	.55	.127		
Grade in which French study began	-.15	.28	.037	.48	.23
IV Learning conditions					
Teacher's perceived listening ability in French	.34	.29	.041		
Frequency of speaking in English in French class	-.40	-.19	.022		
Teacher's perceived ability in French pronunciation	-.01	-.15	.016		
Teacher lived in a French-speaking country	.28	.16	.017		
Frequency of speaking in French in class	.14	.04	.001		
Teacher's perceived ability to read French	.02	-.13	.011		
Frequency of translation work in French class	-.28	-.14	.013		
Years of post-secondary study of French	.23	.08	.004		
Years of teaching foreign languages	.06	.14	.014		
Number of hours spent marking papers	.03	-.15	.018		
Teacher's perceived ability to speak French	.20	-.15	.009		

Number of teachers of French	.22	.04	.002	
Coeducation at Population IV	-.00	-.14	.001	
Examination as an admissions criterion	-.12	-.12	.005	
Teacher's perceived ability to write French	.19	.03	.000	
Sex of teacher	.03	.06	.003	.73 .54
V Kindreds				
Parents help with homework	.29	.31	.085	
Aspiration to understand French	.43	.18	.009	
Total French activities in school	.32	.14	.014	
Years of additional schooling expected	.17	.12	.012	
Parental interest in school	.19	-.18	.017	
Perceived utility of learning French	.30	.08	.002	
Hours of homework	.13	.06	.003	
Interest in French scale	.31	.06	.001	
Hours of reading for pleasure each week	.17	.04	.002	
Aspiration to write French	.34	-.05	.001	
Aspiration to speak French	.41	.05	.001	
Perceived difficulty in learning French compared with other subjects	.18	.02	.000	
		Total	.492	.86 .74

Populations II and IV, respectively. The low relationships between the background variables and performance on the French Listening tests are quite similar to those that were found in French Reading. This undoubtedly reflects the homogeneous sample of students electing to study French. Even when entered first in the regression analyses, the background variables account for only 3% and 4% of the variance in French Listening achievement at Populations II and IV, respectively. The type of program in which the student is enrolled also fails to improve the prediction of French Listening achievement much because virtually all students are enrolled in an academic program.

The variables in the block of time factors, on the other hand, add substantially to the prediction of French Listening achievement. An additional 7% of the variation in French Listening proficiency is accounted for at Population II, and 18% at Population IV. The difference between the population levels is undoubtedly due to the fact that most students at the Population II level are close to the beginning of their study of French and variability on time factors is low.

The results for the block of learning condition variables are similar to those for French Reading, in that almost the same variables enter into the regression analyses for French Listening. The fact that the variables associated with teacher qualifications and competence and with the instructional procedures used in the classroom again emerge as important predictors of achievement in the learning of French underscores their significance. Furthermore, at Population IV, the fact that learning condition variables account for 31% of the variance in French Listening Comprehension has considerable practical importance. To the best of this writer's knowledge, no educational survey has ever demonstrated such a sizable school effect. The reason for this effect is probably due to the fact that, of all subjects studied, French is the one subject that is most clearly a school-learned subject. The results at Population II are not as dramatic. Here an additional 9% of the total variation in school achievement is accounted for by the learning condition variables. This is decidedly less dramatic than the Population IV results, due no doubt to the fact that these are the beginning years of French study. Even here, however, the results are greater than those obtained for Reading Comprehension and Civic Education and roughly similar to those obtained for Science and Literature.

The kindred variables account for an additional 8% and 20% of the variation in French Listening achievement at Populations II and IV, respectively. Again, the variables are virtually the same as those found for French Reading. They are indicative of student interest, attitudes, and motivation to learn French. Interestingly, hours of pleasure reading appears as a concomitant of French Listening achievement only at Population IV; it was not included in the regression analyses at either population level for French Reading. It would seem that a general interest in reading is not an important correlate of achievement in French and that specific interests figure more prominently.

The total amount of variation in French Listening achievement accounted for by the entire set of predictor variables is 27% at Population II and 74% at Population IV. The Population II results are just slightly below those for the other subjects. The explanation for this appears to be the relatively small amount of variability in performance at this level. In contrast, the results at Population IV are dramatic. When one considers the unreliability of the measures, the multiple correlation is as high as can be expected. Student performance in French Listening comprehension is virtually wholly predictable from the set of variables included in the regression analysis.

SUMMARY

The results of the various regression analyses have been summarized in Tables 72 and 73. In general, the results are not very impressive, with the sole exception of French Listening Comprehension at Population IV. The multiple correlations when all variables are included range from .47 for French Reading at Population II to .86 for French Listening at Population IV. 12 of the 14 multiple correlations are between .52 and .65. This means that between 27% and 42% of the variation in achievement between students is accounted for by the full set of predictor variables, kindreds included. This is not an especially impressive result and seems to point up some of the inherent limitations of survey research procedures in detecting effects of various influences on achievement. It may also reflect some lack of variability in the instructional procedures employed in some subjects, notably reading and civic education.

The picture vis-à-vis school effects on learning conditions is rather mixed. Precious little additional variance in student achievement is accounted for by the learning condition variables in Reading Comprehension and Civic Education. Somewhat larger amounts of additional variance in student performance are accounted for in Science and Literature, whereas sizable proportions of additional variance are due to learning conditions in French Reading and Listening. The amount of additional variation in student achievement accounted for by the learning condition variables appears to be a direct

Table 72

Multiple Correlations with Percent Added Variance for Blocks of Variables
for Science, Reading Comprehension, Literature, and Science

					Blocks					
Subject and Population	I		II		III		IV			
	R	% Added Variance	R	% Added Variance	R	% Added Variance	R	% Added Variance		
Science										
I	.42	18	.43	0	.52	9	.59	7		
II	.45	21	.49	3	.55	6	.60	6		
IV	.43	18	.52	9	.59	8	.63	4		
Reading Comprehension										
I	.44	20	.46	1	.50	4	.56	6		
II	.47	22	.51	4	.57	6	.65	11		
IV	.42	17	.51	9	.53	2	.58	6		
Literature										
II	.43	19	.46	2	.53	8	.61	9		
IV	.40	16	.44	4	.50	5	.55	6		
Civic Education										
II	.45	20	.52	7	.55	3	.63	10		
IV	.43	18	.52	9	.56	4	.62	7		

Table 73

Multiple Correlations with Percent Added Variance for Blocks
of Variables for French Reading and French Listening

Subject and Population	I		II		III		IV		V	
	R	% Added Variance	R	% Added Variance	R	% Added Variance	R	% Added Variance	R	% Added Variance
French Reading										
II	.16	3	.18	0	.27	5	.39	7	.47	7
IV	.23	5	.24	1	.36	7	.51	13	.62	13
French Listening										
II	.17	3	.17	0	.31	7	.43	9	.52	8
IV	.19	4	.23	1	.48	19	.73	31	.96	20

function of the extent to which a subject is learned in school. The more the subject is school learned (French is the notable example), the greater the influence of learning conditions in the school. The more the subject is related to both in- and out-of-school experiences, the less the influence of the learning conditions within the school.

Another way of estimating the relative effects of the variables entering into the regression equations for the various subjects at each population level is to examine the unique contribution to R^2 of each variable (i. e., the amount of increase in R^2 that would be obtained if the variable had been entered last in the regression analysis). These unique contributions are almost uniformly low, and the sum of all unique contributions is usually less than one-half of the explained variance in achievement test performance. This suggests the joint effect of the variables both within and among blocks. In practical terms, it suggests that schools are only one of a number of institutions influencing the development of students. The importance of the student's home background is demonstrated in two prominent ways. First, the almost uniformly high relationships between the background variables and student achievement indicate not only the direct influence of the home on the student but also, because of the relatively smaller unique contributions to R^2, the effect indirectly through the kind of schooling he is likely to receive. Second, the generally substantial relationships between the kindred variables and achievement reflect in part the climate and cultural values of the home and the community.

Chapter 9

Epilogue

The IEA Six-Subject Survey is the largest single educational research project ever undertaken. In sheer size, range and number of variables studied, number of countries, schools, teachers, and students involved, the project is unparalleled. The results cannot be easily condensed into a short summary. In fact, this book represents a considerable distillation of a mass of results. Rather than attempt to compress the findings even further, it seems more appropriate to comment on a few issues that grow out of the results.

The conduct of educational research studies on a national level in the United States is an exceedingly difficult enterprise. Unlike many of the participating countries, in which there is a single national system of education and approval by an Education Minister guarantees entry to schools, national studies in the United States must proceed on a district-by-district basis. With over 20,000 autonomous school districts (the sole exception is Hawaii), it is necessary to obtain cooperation from each selected district separately. Given the other commitments of schools, the remarkable accomplishment of the present study was not the amount of non-cooperation but rather the amount of cooperation. The past few years have been difficult ones for schools in the United States as they have attempted to respond to various demands and expectations placed on them. In the light of such circumstances, the willingness to participate in the IEA studies was significant. The sizable body of good will and cooperation coupled with a high degree of commitment to carrying out the field work in a competent and expeditious manner is in large measure responsible for whatever successes the project achieved.

The performance of American students on the various measures of achievement revealed no dramatic results. Students in the United States performed high in some subjects at some levels, average in other subjects at other population levels, and low in other subjects at other levels. In French, performance levels of U.S. students were unquestionably very low. One suspects that this latter finding will not generate great concern. Unlike reading and mathematics, there is no clear sentiment about foreign language learning in the United States. In many European countries, learning a foreign language is seen as necessary for survival; in the United States, it is often viewed as a cultural luxury. Thus the failure to achieve at high levels in French will probably cause little distress.

The performance of American students in the other subjects tested was, as noted, highly varied. In Science, where achievement results were supplemented with teacher ratings on opportunity to learn the material included in the tests, the picture is fairly clear. Students in the United States performed in close accord with the amount of opportunity to learn what was being tested. The implication here is that increased opportunity to learn specific material will lead to higher test performance.

The larger issues raised by the findings, however, are, What can and should be done? Educators have long emphasized that tests measure only a limited number of important outcomes of schooling. Further, the tests employed in the present studies measure a restricted set of outcomes in each school subject. The limited opportunity to learn specific material in science does not mean that American schools are necessarily deficient vis-à-vis the teaching of science or various other subjects. It is possible that different material is being taught and that it is not in some way inferior. The issue is one that will have to be resolved by specialists in the teaching of various subjects. It would seem that detailed study of the actual test items would be a productive enterprise. Determining what should be taught in any academic subject is an extremely important undertaking. Examination of what one group of educators and test developers decided to include in the instruments used in a multinational study would appear to be decidedly worthwhile.

The question of what can be done about the teaching of various school subjects is considerably less clear. Local autonomy in the United States operates to prevent the imposition of a single nationwide curriculum, although there are those who would argue that there is considerably less variability in what is taught than one might think (Smith, 1975). The results of the present study reveal clear regional differences in achievement in the United States, especially between the South and the rest of the country. Furthermore, there is wide variation within each region. Decisions about what will be taught and how it will be taught occur by and large at the local level and, in some cases, even at the individual school and classroom level. The overall achievement of U.S. students in any subject at any level thus represents the effect of literally thousands of local decisions. In many respects, it is difficult to contemplate, let alone discuss, education in the United States as a total system.

Yet there are a number of important findings for the United States. The historical commitment to educating all young people appears to gain support from the results. Unlike Europe, where an economics of scarcity gave rise to a psychology of scarcity, United States schools have sought to give as much education to all for as long as they could profit from it. That such a practice results in a lower average level of performance at the end of high school cannot be denied. There are still sizable numbers of students scoring at the upper levels of the various tests, however. It would seem that a mass system of education can operate to serve virtually all youth and still produce the high levels of achievement needed by society.

The results vis-à-vis differences between predominantly black and predominantly white schools must be viewed with caution. There would appear to be only small differences between the two types of schools with regard to resources but substantial differences in test performance. Although there is considerably greater commitment to equality of educational opportunity in the United States than there was 20 to 30 years ago and although this commitment is, to some extent, expressed in a more equitable distribution of educational resources, it would probably be incorrect to expect that performance differences should be small or non-existent. The American commitment to equality of educational opportunity is a relatively recent one. To expect that differences that existed for generations, sometimes as a result of deliberately discriminatory policies and practices, should suddenly disappear is undoubtedly expecting too much too soon. The differences in social background between the two groups should serve to alert us to the fact that the amelioration of performance differences is not easily accomplished. What would seem to be important is that the commitment to equality of educational opportunity be maintained and extended. The expectation of relatively quick results from such a commitment is unrealistic.

The results of the various regression analyses have been discussed in considerable detail. It is appropriate at this point to comment on some of the major implications that can be drawn. First, the results for each population level within each subject are fairly similar. There are notable differences between subjects, however. If one orders subjects from those that are influenced by both school and non-school factors (Reading Comprehension and Civic Education) to those that are most clearly learned in school (Science and French), there is an increasing amount of variation in student performance accounted for by school variables. This finding seems to add an important qualification to previous research, which typically found little association between variations in school variables and variations in learner achievement.

Furthermore, the increments in performance from one population to another in each subject do show sizable gains. Assertions about schools' not being effective simply have no basis in fact. Even in Reading Comprehension, where little independent variation is accounted for by the school variables, there are substantial gains in achievement from each population level to the next one. Maturation would seem to be a weak explanatory variable for such results.

The second major implication is that the importance of non-school factors must be clearly recognized. Although the way in which the regression analyses were carried out clearly favored the non-school variables, their sizable simple correlations with achievement as well as their prominence in the regression analyses make it impossible to dismiss them. Students enter school in a certain rank order as a result of being born and raised in a certain home and social setting. Schools appear to have little effect in altering this rank ordering. Whether they can do anything to change this involves a set of research questions that go far beyond the scope of this work. At least a generation of programmatic research involving a good deal of careful experimental studies would be needed to even begin to answer the question. Whether schools should be altering the rank ordering among students is a social policy issue that has not been seriously addressed. It would seem that the results of the present study as well as others suggest that schools function to increase the proficiency level of students while maintaining their rank order. The determination of the rank order, at this point, seems to lie beyond the control of the school.

The third major implication stemming from the regression analyses comes not from what was found but rather from what was not found. Considerable effort was made to include a large number of school related variables that were thought to be related to student achievement. A number of these variables are reported in the chapter reporting the results of the regional analyses. Examples of such variables are class size, teacher qualifications, bases for decision making, instructional procedures, assessment practices, and the like. The failure of most of these variables to emerge in the regression analyses in any subject at any level suggests that, within the ranges normally found, they are simply unrelated to achievement. This lack of relationship occurred not only in the United States but in virtually every other country as well. This inability to detect potent instructional variables is somewhat discouraging. It may be that either the variables included in the present study were not the educationally important ones or that survey research methods are inappropriate to the task. Clearly, further study is needed.

References

Blalock, H.M. *Causal inferences in non-experimental research.* Chapel Hill: University of North Carolina Press, 1964.

Bowles, S.; & Levin, H. The determinants of scholastic achievement—an appraisal of some recent evidence. *Journal of Human Resources,* 1968, *3*, 3-24.

Carroll, J.B. *The teaching of French as a foreign language in eight countries.* New York: John Wiley & Sons, 1975.

Coleman, J.S.; *et al. Equality of educational opportunity.* Washington, D.C.: U.S. Department of Health, Education, and Welfare, 1966.

Comber, L.C.; & Keeves, J.P. *Science education in nineteen countries.* New York: John Wiley & Sons, 1973.

Fattu, N. The international math survey: A study marred by distorted publicity. *Phi Delta Kappan,* 1967, *48*, 525-527.

Findley, W.G. The problem of perspective. *Journal for Research in Mathematics Education,* 1971, *2*, 105.

Foshay, A.W., ed. *Educational achievements of thirteen-year-olds in twelve countries.* Hamburg: UNESCO Institute for Education, 1962.

Hogan, T.P. Using old sociometric data for defining norm groups. *Journal of Educational Measurement,* 1970, *7*, 229-232.

Husén, T. *International study of achievement in mathematics: A comparison of twelve countries.* New York: John Wiley & Sons, 1967.

Jencks, C.; *et al. Inequality: A reappraisal of the effect of family and schooling in America.* New York: Basic Books, 1973.

Kerlinger, F.; & Pedhazur, E. *Multiple regression in behavioral research.* New York: Holt, Rinehart & Winston, 1973.

Kish, L. *Survey sampling.* New York: John Wiley & Sons, 1965.

Mayeske, G.W.; *et al. A study of our nation's schools.* Washington, D.C.: U.S. Department of Health, Education, and Welfare, 1969.

Mosteller, F.; & Tukey, J.W. Data analysis, including statistics. In G. Lindzey & E. Aronson, eds., *Handbook of social psychology*, vol. II. Reading, Mass.: Addison-Wesley, 1968.

Passow, A.H.; Noah, H.J.; Eckstein, M.A.; & Mallea, J. *The national case study: An empirical comparative study of twenty-one educational systems.* New York: John Wiley & Sons, 1975.

Peaker, G.F. *An empirical study of education in twenty-one countries: A technical report.* New York: John Wiley & Sons, 1975.

Purves, A.C. *Literature education in ten countries.* New York: John Wiley & Sons, 1973.

Romberg, T.A. Publicity and educational research: A case study. *Journal for Research in Mathematics Education,* 1971, *2*, 132-135.

Smith, M. Commentary, In A. Purves & D. Levine, *Educational policy and international assessment.* Berkeley: McCutchen Publishing Corp., 1975.

Thorndike, R.L. *Reading comprehension education in fifteen countries.* New York: John Wiley & Sons, 1973.

Torney, J.V.; Oppenheim, A.N.; & Farnen, R.F. *Civic education in ten countries: an empirical study.* New York: John Wiley & Sons, 1975.

U.S. Department of Labor. *Dictionary of occupational titles,* 3rd ed. Washington, D.C.: U.S. Government Printing Office, 1965.

9384